Ethnic Islands

THE ASIAN AMERICAN EXPERIENCE

Ethnic Islands

THE EMERGENCE OF
URBAN CHINESE AMERICA

Ronald Takaki

PROFESSOR OF ETHNIC STUDIES
THE UNIVERSITY OF CALIFORNIA AT BERKELEY

Adapted by Rebecca Stefoff

Chelsea House Publishers

New York ✳ Philadelphia

On the cover A street scene in New York's Chinatown.

Chelsea House Publishers

EDITORIAL DIRECTOR   Richard Rennert
EXECUTIVE MANAGING EDITOR   Karyn Gullen Browne
COPY CHIEF   Robin James
PICTURE EDITOR   Adrian G. Allen
ART DIRECTOR   Robert Mitchell
MANUFACTURING DIRECTOR   Gerald Levine

The Asian American Experience

SENIOR EDITOR   Jake Goldberg
SERIES DESIGN   Marjorie Zaum

Staff for *Ethnic Islands*

COPY EDITOR   Joy Sanchez
EDITORIAL ASSISTANT   Kelsey Goss
PICTURE RESEARCHER   Pat Burns

Adapted and reprinted from *Strangers from a Different Shore,*
© 1989 by Ronald Takaki, by arrangement with the author and
Little, Brown and Company, Inc.

Text © 1994 by Ronald Takaki. All rights reserved.
Printed and bound in the United States of America.

First Printing
1   3   5   7   9   8   6   4   2

Library of Congress Cataloging-in-Publication Data
Takaki, Ronald T., 1939–
    Ethnic islands : the emergence of Urban Chinese America / Ronald
Takaki.
        p. cm.—(The Asian American experience)
    Includes bibliographical references and index.
ISBN 0-7910-2180-7
ISBN 0-7910-2280-3 (pbk.)
    1. Chinese Americans—History. 2. China—Emigration and immigra-
tion—History. 3. United States—Emigration and immigration—His-
tory. I. Title. II. Series: Asian American experience (New York, N.Y.)
E184.C5T345 1993
973'.04951—dc20   93-37513
                                                              CIP
                                                              AC

Contents

Since the middle of the 19th century, Chinese immigrants have been helping to create America's multicultural society.

From a Different Shore

AS A CHILD IN HAWAII, I GREW UP IN A MULTICULTURAL corner of America. My own family had roots in Japan and China.

Grandfather Kasuke Okawa arrived in Hawaii in 1866, and my father, Toshio Takaki, came as a 13-year-old boy in 1918. My stepfather, Koon Keu Young, sailed from China to the islands when he was a teenager.

My neighbors were Japanese, Chinese, Hawaiian, Filipino, Portuguese, and Korean. Behind my house, Alice Liu and her friends played the traditional Chinese game of mahjongg late into the night, the clicking of the tiles lulling me to sleep.

Next to us the Miuras flew billowing and colorful carp kites on Japanese boy's day. I heard voices with different accents, different languages, and saw children of different colors.

Together we went barefoot to school and played games like baseball and *jan ken po*. We spoke "pidgin English," a melodious language of the streets and community. "Hey, da kind tako ono, you know," we would say, combining English, Japanese, and Hawaiian. "This octopus is delicious." Racially and culturally diverse, we all thought of ourselves as Americans.

But we did not know why families representing such an array of nationalities from different shores were living together and sharing their cultures and a common language. Our teachers and textbooks did not explain the diversity of our community or the sources of our unity.

After graduation from high school, I attended a college in a midwestern town where I found myself invited to "dinners for foreign students" sponsored by local churches and clubs like the Rotary. I politely tried to explain to my kind hosts that I was not a "foreign student." My fellow students and even my professors would ask me how long I had been in America and where I had learned to speak English. "In this country," I would reply. And sometimes I would add: "I was born in America, and my family has been here for three generations."

Asian Americans have been here for over 150 years. They are diverse, coming originally from countries such as China, Japan, Korea, the Philippines, India, Vietnam, Laos, and Cambodia. Many of them live in Chinatowns, the colorful streets filled with sidewalk vegetable stands and crowds of people carrying shopping bags; their communities are also called Little Tokyo, Koreatown, and Little Saigon. Asian Americans work in hot kitchens and bus tables in restaurants with elegant names like Jade Pagoda and Bombay Spice. In garment factories, Chinese and Korean women hunch over whirling sewing machines, their babies sleeping nearby on blankets. In the Silicon Valley of California, rows and rows of Vietnamese and Laotian women serve as the eyes and hands of production assembly lines for computer chip industries. Tough Chinese gang members strut on Grant Avenue in San Francisco and Canal Street in New York's Chinatown. In La Crosse, Wisconsin, Hmong refugees from Laos, now dependent on welfare, sit and stare at the snowdrifts outside their windows. Asian American engineers do complex research in the laboratories of the high-technology industries along

Route 128 in Massachusetts. Asian Americans seem to be everywhere on university campuses.

Today, Asian Americans belong to the fastest growing ethnic group in the United States. Kept out of the United States by immigration restriction laws in the 19th and early 20th centuries, Asians have recently been coming again to America. The 1965 immigration act reopened the gates to immigrants from Asia, allowing 20,000 immigrants from each country to enter every year. In the early 1990s, half of all immigrants entering annually are Asian.

The growth of the Asian American population has been dramatic: In 1960, there were only 877,934 Asians in the United States, representing a mere one half of 1% of the American people. Thirty years later, they numbered about seven million, or 3% of the population. They included 1,645,000 Chinese, 1,400,000 Filipinos, 845,000 Japanese, 815,000 Asian Indians, 800,000 Koreans, 614,000 Vietnamese, 150,000 Laotians, 147,000 Cambodians, and 90,000 Hmong. By the year 2000, Asian Americans will probably represent 4% of the total United States population. In California, Asian Americans already make up 10% of the state's inhabitants, compared with 7.5% for African Americans.

Yet very little is known about Asian Americans and their history. Many existing history books give Asian Americans only passing notice—or overlook them entirely. "When one hears Americans tell of the immigrants who built this nation," Congressman Norman Mineta of California observed, "one is often led to believe that all our forebearers came from Europe. When one hears stories about the pioneers going West to shape the land, the Asian immigrant is rarely mentioned."

Indeed, many history books have equated "American" with "white" or "European" in origin. In his prize-winning study, *The Uprooted*, Harvard historian Oscar Handlin presented—to use the book's subtitle—"the Epic Story of the Great Migrations that Made the American People." But Handlin's "epic story" completely left out the "uprooted" from lands across the Pacific Ocean and the "great migrations" from Asia that also helped to make "the American people." As Americans, we have origins in Europe, the Americas, Africa, and also Asia.

We need to include Asians in the history of America. How and why, we ask in this series, were the experiences of these various groups—Chinese, Japanese, Korean, Filipino, Asian Indian, and Southeast Asian—similar to and different from each other? Comparing the experiences of different nationalities can help us see what events were particular to a group and also highlight the experiences they all shared.

Why did Asian immigrants leave everything they knew and loved to come to a strange world so far away? They were "pushed" by hardships in the homelands and "pulled" by demands for their labor in Canada, Brazil, and especially the United States. But what were their own fierce dreams— from the first enterprising Chinese miners of the 1850s in search of "Gold Mountain" to the recent refugees fleeing frantically on helicopters and leaking boats from the ravages of war in Vietnam?

Besides their points of origin, we need to examine the experiences of Asian Americans in different geographical regions, especially Hawaii compared with the mainland. The time of arrival also shaped their lives and communities. About one million people entered the United States between the California gold rush of 1849 and the 1924 immigration act that cut off the flow of peoples from Asian countries. After a break of some 40 years, a second group numbering about four million came between 1965 and 1990. How do we compare the two waves of Asian immigration?

To answer our questions in these volumes, we must study Asian Americans as men and women with minds, wills, and voices. By "voices" we mean their own words and stories as told in their oral histories, conversations, speeches, and songs as well as their own writings—diaries, letters, newspapers, novels, and poems. We need to know the ordinary people.

So much of history has been the story of kings and elites, as if the "little people" were invisible and voiceless. An Asian American told an interviewer: "I am a second generation Korean American without any achievements in life and I have no education. What is it you want to hear from me? My life is not worth telling to anyone." Similarly, a Chinese immigrant said: "You know, it seems to me there's no use in me telling you all this! I was just a simple worker, a farm worker around here. My story is not going to interest anybody." But others realize they are worthy of attention. "What is it you want to know?" an old Filipino immigrant asked a researcher. "Talk about history. What's that . . . ah, the story of my life . . . and how people lived with each other in my time."

Their stories can enable us to understand Asians as actors in the making of history and as people entitled to dignity. "I hope this survey do a lot of good for Chinese people," a Chinese man told an interviewer from Stanford

University in the 1920s. "Make American people realize that Chinese people are humans. I think very few American people really know anything about Chinese." Elderly Asians want the younger generations to know about their experiences. "Our stories should be listened to by many young people," said a 91-year-old retired Japanese plantation laborer. "It's for their sake. We really had a hard time, you know."

The stories of Asian immigrations belong to our country's history. They need to be recorded in our history books, for they reflect the making of America as a nation of immigrants, as a place where men and women came to find a new beginning. At first, many Asian immigrants—probably most of them—saw themselves as sojourners, or temporary migrants. Like many European immigrants such as the Italians and Greeks, they came to America thinking they would be here only a short time. They had left their wives and children behind in their homelands. Their plan was to work here for a few years and then return home with money. But, after their arrival, many found themselves staying. They became settlers instead of remaining sojourners. Bringing their families to their adopted country, they began putting down new roots in America.

But, coming here from Asia, many of America's immigrants found they were not allowed to feel at home in the United States. Even their grandchildren and great-grandchildren still find they are not viewed and accepted as Americans. "We feel that we're a guest in someone else's house," said third generation Ron Wakabayashi, National Director of the Japanese American Citizens League, "that we can never really relax and put our feet on the table."

Behind Wakabayashi's complaint is the question: Why have Asian Americans been considered outsiders? America's immigrants from Pacific shores found they were forced to remain strangers in the new land. Their experiences here were profoundly different from the experiences of European immigrants. Asian immigrants had qualities they could not change or hide—the shape of their eyes, the color of their hair, the complexion of their skins. They were subjected not only to cultural and ethnic prejudice but also to racism. Unlike the Irish and other groups from Europe, Asian immigrants were not treated as individuals but as members of a group with distinctive physical characteristics. Regardless of their personal merits, they sadly discovered, they could not gain acceptance in the larger society.

Unlike European immigrants, Asians were victimized by laws and policies that discriminated on the basis of race. The Chinese Exclusion Act of 1882 barred the Chinese from coming to America because they were Chinese. The National Origins Act of 1924 totally prohibited Japanese immigration.

The laws determined not only who could come to America but also who could become citizens. Decades before Asian immigration began, the United States had already defined the complexion of its citizens: the Naturalization Law of 1790 had specified that naturalized citizenship was to be reserved for "whites." This law remained in effect until 1952. Unlike white ethnic immigrants from countries like Ireland, Asian immigrants were denied citizenship and also the right to vote.

But America also had an opposing tradition and vision, springing from the reality of racial and cultural "diversity." Ours has been, as Walt Whitman celebrated so lyrically, "a teeming Nation of nations" composed of a "vast, surging, hopeful army of workers," a new society where all should be welcomed, "Chinese, Irish, German,—all, all, without exceptions." In the early 20th century, a Japanese immigrant described in poetry a lesson that had been learned by farm laborers of different nationalities—Japanese, Filipino, Mexican, and Asian Indian:

> *People harvesting*
> *Work together unaware*
> *Of racial problems.*

A Filipino immigrant laborer in California expressed a similar hope and understanding. America was, Macario Bulosan told his brother Carlos, "not a land of one race or one class of men" but "a new world" of respect and unconditional opportunities for all who toiled and suffered from oppression, from "the first Indian that offered peace in Manhattan to the last Filipino pea pickers." Asian immigrants came here, as one of them expressed it, searching for "a door into America" and seeking "to build a new life with untried materials." He asked: "Would it be possible for an immigrant like me to become a part of the American dream?"

This series invites students to learn how Asian Americans belong to the larger story of the rich multicultural mosaic called the United States of America.

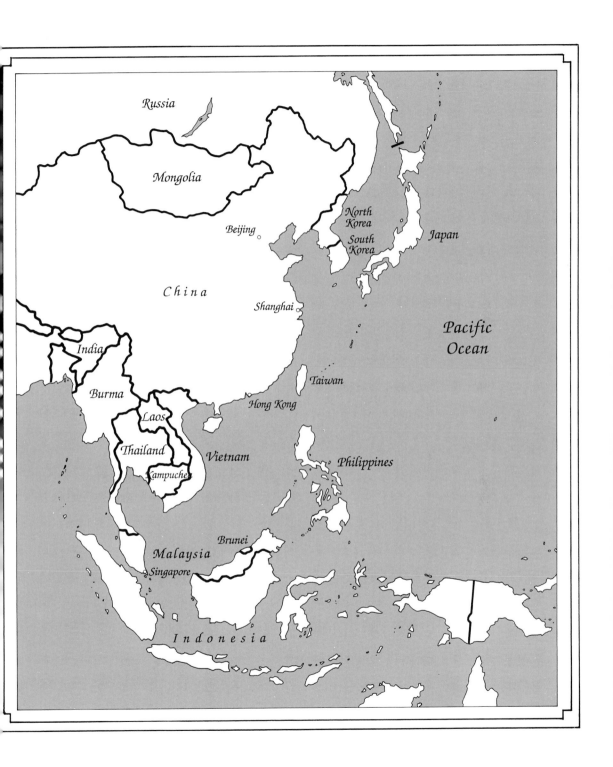

A group of Chinese and white miners in 19th-century California.

Chapter One

The Gold Mountain Men

MANY YEARS AGO, AROUND THE END OF THE 19TH century, a Chinese man in Oregon began writing a letter to his wife in far-off China. He headed the letter "My Beloved Wife" and then wrote:

> It has been several autumns now since your dull husband left you for a far remote alien land. Thanks to my hearty body I am all right. Therefore stop your embroidering worries about me.
>
> Yesterday I received another of your letters. I could not keep tears from running down my cheeks when thinking about the miserable and needy circumstances of our home, and thinking back to the time of our separation.
>
> Because of our destitution I went out, trying to make a living. Who could know that the Fate is always opposite to man's design? Because I can get no gold, I am detained in this secluded corner of a strange land. . . . I wish this paper would console you a little. This is all what I can do for now. . . .

The letter was never finished and never mailed. It was later found in a drawer in a Chinese store in central Oregon. The sad and lonely writer of the letter was one of the thousands of Chinese men who came to America in the 19th century to seek their fortunes.

In southern China, the birthplace of most of these immigrants, California was called *Gam Saan*, which means "Gold Mountain." The name was given to California during the Gold Rush of 1849, when the first Chinese prospectors crossed the Pacific Ocean to pan for gold in the California hills. These hopeful travelers were called the Gold Mountain

Men. In the years that followed, the Gold Mountain Men
moved from mining into other kinds of labor and business.
They worked on farms and in factories; they helped build
railroads across the West; and they opened stores, hotels, and
restaurants in many American cities. Even after they left the
gold fields, America continued to be envisioned as a "Gold
Mountain," a place where a poor man could earn enough
money to return home to his family in triumph.

Between the 1840s and the 1920s, about 380,000
Chinese immigrants came to the United States, and nearly all
of them were men. Many, perhaps most, of them left their
wives and families in China because they planned to stay in
America only until they had saved some money. Their futures
seemed promising when they left their villages for Gold
Mountain. A Chinese folk song said

> *If you have a daughter, marry her quickly to a
>   traveller to Gold Mountain,*
> *For when he gets off the boat, he will bring
>   hundreds of pieces of silver.*

But many of the Gold Mountain Men found that their
dreams of wealth did not come true. Some failed to strike
gold. They went into debt and could not afford their passage
home. Others, desperate for a little pleasure in their hard-
working lives, lost their savings through gambling or drinking.
They told themselves, "Next year I will have enough money.
Next year I will be able to go home." Meanwhile, the years
passed, and the return to China was delayed again and again.
Some of the Gold Mountain Men now remembered another
folk rhyme, one that held a warning:

If you have a daughter, do not marry her to a
     traveller to Gold Mountain,
For he will leave her and forget her.

Back in China, wives longed for the warmth and
presence of their men who were far away in the land of Gold
Mountain. One of their songs told of their loneliness:

You bid farewell to the village well, setting out for
     overseas.
It's been eight years, or is it already ten, and
     you haven't thought of home.
Willow branches are now brilliant, fields exuberantly
     green.
In her bedroom, the young woman's bosom is filled with
     frustration and grief.

*William H. Jackson, one of
the foremost photographers of
the early West, captured
this 1870 image of Chinese
miners surrounded by the vast
Montana landscape.*

These women had become "widows" of men living in America. They sent their husbands "letters of love, soaked with tears." The nameless writer of the unfinished letter in Oregon received such a message of love and tears from his wife. Sadly, he could only tell her that he did not have the money to come home.

The owners of the store where this letter was found had similar experiences. They were two Chinese men who had come to America in the 1880s, planning to work for a while and then return to China. Gradually, over the years, as they built their business and developed ties to their new community, they felt themselves growing apart from their homeland and their families. In 1899, one of the men, Lung On, received a letter from his father:

> Come home as soon as you can. Don't say 'no' to me any more. . . . You are my only son. You have no brothers and your age is near forty. . . . You have been away from home for seventeen years, you know nothing about our domestic situation. . . . Come back, let our family be reunited and enjoy the rest of our lives.

Lung's wife also urged her absent mate to return, and she scolded him for the way he was living in America. She wrote:

> According to Mr. Wang, you are indulging in sensuality, and have no desire to return home. On hearing this I am shocked and pained. I have been expecting your return day after day. . . . But, alas, I don't know what kind of substance your heart is made of. . . . Your daughter is now at the age of betrothal and it is your responsibility to arrange her marriage.

Finally, in 1905, Lung On wrote to his cousin that he was still planning to come back to China "as soon as I accumulate enough money to pay the fare." But a few weeks later, Lung received a letter from his cousin and learned that events in the life of his family in China had already passed him by. The letter said:

> Two years ago your mother died. Last year your daughter married. Your aged father is immobile. He will pass away any time now. Your wife feels left out and hurt. . . . Come back as soon as you receive this message.

Meanwhile, Lung's partner had also received a letter from his father, who wrote, "Men go abroad so that they might make money for support of their families, but you have sent neither money nor a letter since you left."

Unable or unwilling to return to China, the Chinese immigrants in America lived in a world of men. Most of them had wives in China, but in America they became "bachelors." Separated from their families in China, they missed the company of their own sons and daughters, the sounds and laughter of children. Perhaps this was why Lung On and his partner saved pictures of children cut from calendars, advertisements, and newspapers, and placed them safely in a box. Discovered decades later in a desk drawer in the abandoned store, this box of pictures suggested the sadness of the Chinese immigrant fathers who lived so far from their children. The two shopkeepers also pampered the white children in the neighborhood. One of these children recalled years later that the shopkeepers always gave her "Chinese candy, oranges and other goodies."

*Bemused passengers watch
Chinese railway workers
eat their lunch near Missoula,
Montana. In the early days
of Asian immigration, most
white Americans had never met
Chinese people; to them, the
newcomers from China
seemed quaint and exotic.*

Back home, Chinese women studied old, yellowing photographs of their men, so young and so handsome. Look at these dreamers and the twinkle in their eyes, filled with possibilities and promises, they said proudly. But what did they look like now, after 20 years in Gold Mountain? A folk song told of the widening distances between Chinese men in America and their wives in China:

> *Pitiful is the twenty-year sojourner,*
> *Unable to make it home.*
> *Having been everywhere—north, south, east,*
> *west—*
> *Always obstacles along the way, pain*
> *knitting my brows.*
> *Worried, in silence.*
> *Ashamed, wishes unfulfilled.*

A reflection on the mirror, a sudden fright:
  hair, half frost-white.
Frequent letters from home, all filled with much
  complaint.

The women struggled with loneliness at home, but in America the men faced a struggle of their own: the fight against prejudice. At first the Chinese workers had been welcomed in California and elsewhere. Their contributions to American agriculture and industry were initially recognized. But as white workers began to see the Chinese immigrants as competitors for jobs, they turned their hostility and frustration against the newcomers in outbreaks of racial violence. As the 19th century drew to a close, economic conditions in the United States began to change. The growth of business and industry slowed, and there were not enough jobs to go around.

Sojourners in America often sent their relatives in China photographs that showed how well they lived in "Gold Mountain." The sewing machine and bicycle are signs of prosperity.

Few women and children came from China in the first wave of immigration.
Far from their wives and families, many of the immigrant men led lonely,
empty lives.

Unemployment was a new problem in America. Economic hard times fueled a backlash against the Chinese immigrants.

The Chinese residents of the United States were not completely without rights. An 1868 treaty between China and the United States said that the civil rights of Chinese people living in America must be protected, and further protection was granted by the federal Civil Rights Act of 1870. But the Chinese immigrants were barred from United States citizenship by a 1790 law that said that only "white" immigrants could become citizens. This law meant that the thousands of Chinese immigrants who lived and worked in America could never become citizens. They were doomed to remain forever strangers because of their race.

Racism was a growing problem for the Chinese in America during the final decades of the 19th century. The economic depression of the 1880s brought unemployment and competition for jobs, and the Chinese immigrants became scapegoats—they were blamed for America's economic problems. There were anti-Chinese riots in many American cities, and Chinese people were driven out of communities, beaten, and killed.

This national mood of racial hostility toward the Chinese led to a demand for laws against immigration from China. In 1882, Congress passed the Chinese Exclusion Act, which banned the entry of Chinese laborers. Two years later, in a lawsuit called the *Ah Moy* case, an American court ruled that the Chinese laborers who were already in the United States could not bring their wives from China to join them. This court decision prevented most Chinese women from entering the United States. Together, the Exclusion Act and

A Chinese Mexican family. With few Chinese women available for marriage in the United States, some of the immigrants found wives outside their ethnic group.

the *Ah Moy* decision ended almost all immigration from China.

Not all Americans agreed that Chinese immigrants should be kept out of the country. Jacob Riis, a reporter and social reformer, discussed the question of Chinese immigration in his important 1890 book *How the Other Half Lives.* "Rather than banish the Chinaman," Riis wrote, "I would have the door opened wider—for his wife; make it a condition of his coming or staying that he bring his wife with him. Then, at least, he might not be what he now is and remains, a homeless stranger among us." But the door to Chinese immigration had already been closed by the American government. Chinese laborers in the United States could stay, but no more could come. As a result, Chinese communities in America stopped growing, and the great majority of the immigrants realized that they were forever separated from their wives and families.

Desperate to be reunited with their loved ones, some men looked for loopholes in the law. There were several such loopholes. Federal law allowed Chinese men who were U.S. citizens to bring their wives to the United States. This loophole did not help very many Chinese men, however, because the 1790 federal law prevented immigrants from becoming citizens. The only Chinese people who were U.S. citizens were those who had been born in the United States. And because so few Chinese women had come to America, the number of Chinese babies born in the United States was quite small.

Another legal loophole was more promising. Under the Exclusion Act, laborers were forbidden to bring their relatives into the United States, but Chinese merchants—importers, store owners, and businessmen—were permitted to send for their families. As a result, many Chinese laundry workers, restaurant owners, and even common laborers tried to pose as "paper merchants," with papers that claimed they were the owners of merchant businesses. A Chinese man who had sworn an oath to the immigration authorities that he was a merchant turned out to be a hotel cook; another was really a gardener. Other Chinese workers bribed merchants to list them as partners, or bought shares in businesses in order to claim that they were merchants.

Most Chinese men, however, believed they would never be able to bring their wives to America. As the 20th century began, they were resigned to living out their lives in "bachelor" communities and to watching the Chinese presence in America dwindle and fade away. Suddenly, however, a natural disaster changed the course of Chinese American history. One of the biggest catastrophes in American history opened the way for a new wave of Chinese immigration.

The Angel Island Immigration Station was built on an island
in San Francisco Bay to handle the rush of immigrants to the city after
the great earthquake of 1906.

EARLY IN THE MORNING OF APRIL 18, 1906, AN EARTH-quake shook San Francisco. In the city's Chinatown, people screamed, "The earth dragon is wriggling." In terror, they jumped out of their beds, fled from collapsing buildings, and ran down buckling streets. "I remember how everything fell off the shelf," recalled a Chinese American woman who was seven years old when the earthquake struck. "We had one of those stoves made out of brick and the stove had crumbled. So my father was going to put it back together again. But very soon we had to evacuate the place."

Another resident of Chinatown was asleep when the earthquake hit. He said, "I wake up, and here everything is shaking. Then here went everything tumbling down!" He looked out onto California Street and saw "a big crack" in the earth. Then came the fires, roaring down Montgomery Street and through the financial district.

The earthquake itself was felt all along the California coast, from Los Angeles in the south to the Oregon border in the north. In San Francisco, it toppled buildings and tore streets apart. Fires caused by overturned lanterns and stoves were even more destructive than the quake itself. They reduced much of the city to charred rubble. More than 700 people were killed in the quake and the fires that followed. Thousands more were left homeless; they camped on the sand dunes west of San Francisco or made their way to smaller towns outside the city. By the time the fires subsided, San Francisco had suffered more than $400 million worth of damages.

The fires, more than the actual quake, had a profound effect on the Chinese population in America. Flames destroyed almost all of the city records of San Francisco, which

The dining hall at Angel Island. For many immigrants, the first experience of America was a period of confinement in the crowded, impersonal station.

was the main port of entry for immigrants from China and the site of the largest Chinatown in America. Once the city's files of birth certificates had been turned to ashes, Chinese men could claim that they had been born in San Francisco, and there was no way for authorities to disprove their claims. Being born in San Francisco meant that they were U.S. citizens, and as citizens they could bring their wives to the United States. The earthquake thus opened the way for Chinese women to enter the country again.

Before the earthquake, 5% or less of the Chinese population had been women. But after the catastrophe in San Francisco, more women began arriving—from 219 in 1910 to 1,893 in 1924. During this time, 25% of Chinese immigrants were female. Altogether, more than 10,000 Chinese women entered the United States between 1907 and 1924. By 1930, 20% of all Chinese people in America were women. Chinese communities in America were no longer mostly male worlds. Chinese American families could now take root.

Chinese sons also began coming to America. By law, the children of U.S. citizens were also citizens, even if they were born in a foreign country. If a Chinese man who was an American citizen visited China and fathered a child there, that child was an American citizen by birth and was allowed to enter the United States. Many young men came to the United States as sons of American citizens of Chinese ancestry. Others came as imposters, called "paper sons." They bought or forged the birth certificates of American citizens born in China and then claimed they were citizens in order to enter the United States.

A Chinese American man explained how the "paper son" process worked: "In the beginning my father came in as a laborer. But the 1906 earthquake came along and destroyed all those immigration things. So that was a big chance for a lot of Chinese. They forged themselves certificates saying they were born in this country, and then when the time came, they could go back to China and bring back four or five sons, just like that!" Exactly how many Chinese men falsely claimed citizenship as paper sons will never be known, but if every claim to citizenship were true, each of the Chinese women who lived in San Francisco before 1906 would have had to have borne 800 children!

The possession of a birth certificate did not mean automatic entry into the United States, however. In 1910, to cope with the flood of new arrivals from China, the U.S.

government set up an immigration station at Angel Island in the San Francisco Bay. There, the paper sons were held until they could prove their American identity. They were tested on their knowledge of their so-called families. To prepare for these examinations, they studied crib sheets during the voyage across the Pacific Ocean from China, memorizing all sorts of facts about the families to which they claimed to belong. They had to remember the names and birthdays of everyone in the family, as well as details about marriages, deaths, and family

Flames sweep through San Francisco's Chinatown in the aftermath of the great earthquake of April 1906. The number of deaths in Chinatown is unknown, but scores of charred bodies were found among the ruins.

histories. As their ships approached the Golden Gate, the paper sons tore up their crib sheets and threw them overboard.

Paper son Jim Quock said that his grandfather had gone to America in the 1860s and had accumulated a fortune in gold. But he was robbed and murdered. "They never found the body or anything," Quock said. In the hope of making money in America, Quock decided to follow his grandfather's path. "The only way I could ccme was to buy a paper, buy a citizen paper," he said. "I paid quite a bit of money, too. I paid $102 gold!" Quock was given a 200-page book about his paper family to study. After arriving at the Angel Island Immigration Station, he was detained for three weeks while officials questioned him. "They ask you questions like how many steps in your house?" Quock recalled. "Your house had a clock? Where do you sleep at your house? I said, 'I sleep with my grandmother and brother.' They say, 'Okay, which position do you sleep?' All kinds of questions; you got to think."

Sometimes paper sons had to think quickly during the examination. Two young men, seeking admission as the sons of a merchant, were questioned by the inspectors. The first young man was asked if the family had a dog, and he answered, "Yes." Later, the second man was asked the same question and he said, "No, no dog." The inspectors then called back the first young man, pressing him about the existence of the dog. "Yes," he replied smartly, "well, we had a dog, but we knew we were coming to the United States, so we ate the dog."

The presence of paper sons often led to confusing situations in families. A father named Wong could have two real sons, each with a "paper name" because each had entered as the paper son of a different man. A Mr. Lee could enter the country as "Mr. Woo." His wife would use the name "Mrs. Woo," and his children would register for school and the selective service as Woos. But to their family and in the Chinese community they would be Lees. Chinese people would often explain their names by saying, "According to the paper, I am supposed to be his brother" or "I share the same paper with him."

Sen Hin Yung, who entered America as the 16-year-old son of a merchant in 1921, was actually Yip Jing Tom. On his gravestone, Yip Jing Tom is written in Chinese and Sen Hin Yung in English. Another immigrant, Bing Mak, arrived in San Francisco in January 1910. He passed the examination at Angel Island and was admitted to America as Bing Lai, the son of his mother's cousin, Poon Lai. Ack Pon Yee, the nephew of Boston merchant Tze Chun Wong, came to the United States as his uncle's paper son. One of Wong's sons had died as a baby, and Ack Pon Yee filled the slot as a Wong.

There was a paper son in our family. My stepfather Koon Keu Young entered America as the son of merchant; then his father went back to China and died there. Many years later a "Cousin Bobby" appeared at our house. As a child I was told he was my stepfather's cousin, the son of another merchant. Cousin Bobby was a cook and he often helped in our family restaurant. The two cousins were very close; I can still remember them telling stories loudly in Cantonese and laughing as they flashed their spatulas over sizzling woks. After I had graduated from college, I was surprised to learn from my stepfather that the two men were actually brothers. So "Cousin Bobby" became "Uncle Bobby." Because his father had not been a U.S. citizen, Bobby was unable to enter

the United States, and so he had had to pretend to be another man's son.

Thanks to the San Francisco earthquake, Chinese immigrants once again entered the United States in the early 20th century. They came in the thousands. After sailing through the Golden Gate and getting off their ships at Angel Island, the newcomers were placed in barracks at the immigration station. Their quarters were crowded and unsanitary, like a slum. "When we arrived," said one of them, "they locked us up like criminals in compartments like the cages in the zoo. They counted us and then took us upstairs to our rooms. There were two to three rooms in the women's section. . . . Each of the rooms could fit twenty or thirty persons." The

The earthquake and fires tore swaths through downtown San Francisco. Very soon afterward, however, the city—including Chinatown—was rebuilt, bigger and busier than ever.

men were placed in one large room. There were 190 "small boys up to old men, all together in the same room," a visitor reported in 1922. "Some were sleeping in the hammock-like beds with their belongings hanging in every possible way . . . while others were smoking or gambling."

The days at Angel Island were long and boring. The lights were turned out around 9:00 P.M., but many of the Chinese immigrants could not fall asleep. Through the barrack windows they could see San Francisco to the west and Oakland to the east—close, but still out of reach. The travelers had journeyed so far to come to America, and yet they had not been allowed to enter. As they waited and waited, many expressed their rage and frustration in poems carved on the walls of the barracks:

> *Imprisoned in the wooden building day after*
> *day,*
> *My freedom withheld; how can I bear to talk*
> *about it?*
> *The days are long and the bottle constantly*
> *empty; my sad mood, even so, is not*
> *dispelled.*
> *Nights are long, and the pillow cold; who can*
> *pity my loneliness?*

The newcomers were not released until they had convinced the authorities that they were really entitled to citizenship. Not everyone passed the examinations. About one in ten was sent back to China.

> *Barred from land, I really am to be pitied.*
> *My heart trembles at being deported back to*

China. . . .
I came to seek wealth but instead reaped
poverty.

Some, in anger, vowed revenge. They promised in their poems, still defiantly visible on the walls of the barracks, to punish the "barbarians," "the heartless white devils," and destroy the racial barriers of exclusion.

It is unbearable to relate the stories
accumulated on the Island slopes.
Wait till the day I become successful and
fulfill my wish!
I will not speak of love when I level the
immigration station!

The lucky ones were allowed to hurry onto ferries and sail happily to San Francisco. By 1943, some 50,000 Chinese men and women had entered America through Angel Island. Gladly leaving the grim immigration station behind, they made their way to the cities, seeking shelter and employment in Chinatowns.

A Chinese laundry in Arizona served Native American patrons.
Forced to become self-employed, many Chinese immigrants turned
to the laundry business.

THE EARLIEST CHINESE IMMIGRANTS HAD WORKED primarily in the countryside, as miners, railroad builders, or farm laborers. But in the early decades of the 20th century, the Chinese population in America became concentrated in large urban centers, where they worked in restaurants, laundries, and garment factories. The largest Chinese communities were in the West; more than half of all Chinese people in America lived in the Pacific states. Another one-fifth of the Chinese population lived in the Middle Atlantic states, including New York. The first Chinese immigrants had spread into the Rocky Mountain states, building Chinatowns in cities such as Butte, Montana; Boise, Idaho; Denver, Colorado; and Salt Lake City, Utah. But these Chinatowns declined between 1900 and 1940, while Chinese communities in San Francisco, New York City, and other large coastal cities continued to grow. By 1940, 91% of the Chinese population in the United States was classified by the U.S. Census Bureau as "urban." (In comparison, 57% of the total U.S. population lived in cities in 1940.) The Chinese in America had become city-dwellers.

One reason the small-town Chinatowns declined was the shortage of women, who were kept out by the exclusion laws. A Chinese American man described the disappearance of the Chinese community in Sebastopol, California, this way: "Well, there they were, with three hundred Chinese workers, and except for my mother, not a single woman. That was the whole Chinese settlement in Sebastopol. All those old guys thought about was how they wanted to go back to China. . . . And the reason there's no Chinese in Sebastopol today is that eventually they all died off because there was no reproduction."

As the Chinese population in the small towns dwindled, Chinese were drawn to the big cities where they could find jobs. These jobs were very different from the work that Chinese laborers had done in the 19th century. At that time, Chinese laborers had been busy in every part of the American economy: agriculture, mining, manufacturing, and transportation. But by 1920, they had virtually vanished from these areas of employment. Chinese farm laborers had been the mainstay of California's agriculture in the late 19th century, but in 1920 Chinese workers did less than 1% of the harvesting. By then, there were only 150 Chinese miners, compared with 17,600 in 1870. Only 100 Chinese workers were employed making cigars, boots, and shoes, compared with more than 2,000 in 1870. Fewer than 500 Chinese people were railroad workers in 1920, compared with more than 10,000 who had been employed by the Central Pacific Railroad in the 1860s.

The 20th-century Chinese immigrants and their children found themselves in a different kind of labor market. More than half of them worked in services, mostly restaurant and laundry work. They had been driven out of the general labor market by racial prejudice and forced to withdraw to the Chinese ethnic economy, working in Chinese-owned businesses. "In all my life," said Peter Wong, who immigrated in 1921, "I always worked for the Chinese, never for Americans. I worked in a laundry, I worked in a restaurant, I worked in a Chinese store."

One white worker summed up a common attitude toward Chinese people, saying, "The Chinks are all right if they remain in their place. I don't mind their working in the laundry business, but they should not go any higher than that. After all, there aren't even enough jobs for us whites, without them butting in." Many Chinese people did indeed find work in laundries. Explaining why so many of them had entered the laundry business, one Chinese man said, "It is a very hard job, sure enough. But there is nothing else to do. This is the kind of life we have to take in America. I, as one of the many, do not like to work in the laundry, but what else can I do? You've got to take it; that's all."

The "Chinese laundry" was invented in America—it did not exist in China, where there were no commercial laundries and women did the family washing at home. In America, however, Chinese men were forced into this untraditional occupation because it was one of the few avenues open to them. Opening a small laundry did not require a great deal of money, and with hard work it would provide a modest living. So the "Chinese laundry" became a familiar sight in American cities and towns, although the only thing Chinese about these laundries was the people who operated them. They used the same equipment and methods as American laundries, and many of the Chinese laundrymen learned their trade from Americans.

The number of Chinese laundries soared in the first half of the 20th century. In Chicago, for example, there were 209 of them in 1903 and 704 in 1928. By 1940, New York City had Chinese laundries "located on almost every street corner." By 1920, more than a quarter of all working Chinese people in America were laundry workers (compared with only 8% in 1870).

Chinese laundrymen found they had to spread themselves out, to Chicago, New York, Baltimore, Los Angeles, and other cities, and to different districts within a city, where there were not too many laundries. "If you are the only laundry

located in the country or small city, people will bring their clothes to you," said a laundry operator. "If there were two laundries, you will not find enough to eat."

Running a laundry was hard work. First, the laundryman had to get some money to start the business—this was often borrowed from relatives. For example, one laundryman's accounts for 1927 show that for a new shop he had borrowed

$100 from Cousin T. H., $100 from Uncle H. K., $20 from Uncle S. K., and $20 from Cousin W. T. The money to start a laundry could also come from the *woi,* a sort of "loan of the month club." Meaning "get together" or "put together," the woi was a collective loan fund organized by a family or clan group of 15 to 30 members. The woi was one of the main ways for Chinese entrepreneurs to finance their laundries. Each member placed an equal amount of money into a pool at the beginning of the first month of the year, and the total sum was then loaned to a member. This was repeated each month for a year. Every member made his regular contribution, and members with loans added the interest due. In this way, a dozen different men could get loans in a year.

Once he had obtained his loan and opened his business, the Chinese laundryman found himself working long hours. A Chinese American researcher recorded the daily activities of Tong, a laundryman, and his partners. Like most laundrymen, they lived in the back of the shop, and they woke early in the morning. At 8:00 A.M., Tong was going out to collect the laundry. Hong and Wah were working inside. The steam boiler was working and the washtub was moving. Ming was alone in the office where he sorted and marked the laundry that customers had just brought in. The noise of the washing machine drowned out their conversation.

Tong returned with a load of dirty laundry in a wooden trunk and left again. The first wash was done, and Hong and Wah rinsed and wrung it, then hung it to dry. About 10:00 A.M., the wheel of the washing machine turned again. Tong was back, bringing a second load with him. From the washing machine to the wash tub to the wringing machine and the drying rooms took about one hour and a half. Around

10:30 A.M., Hong began to cook lunch. For lunch on busy days, the laundrymen had cold meats and cakes with coffee. In the afternoon, they turned to the next set of tasks: Hong did most of the starching work, with the help of Ming. Wah and Tong did the damping and ironing. Afterward, Hong set the collars and cuffs on a machine, a chore that took him the whole afternoon and deep into the night. At 11:30 at night, all the men ate their dinner. After supper, they all sat out in the yard to cool off before they went to bed. But they did not get to sleep until 1:00 A.M.

A retired laundry operator sighed, "Ah, those days were hard ones. It is very hard to work at the laundry." Referring to the weight of the heavy iron, he added, "They don't call it 'Eight Pound Livelihood' for nothing." Filled with red-hot charcoal, the iron seemed to be a symbol of burdensome toil. Laundrymen had to stand all day. "My feet bothered me," an old man said. "I could no longer stand too long on my feet." But even younger men felt the daily wear and tear on their bodies. "I don't like this kind of life; it is not human life. To be a laundryman is to be just a slave. I work because I have to," one of them moaned. "I feel backaches all the time and headaches. I am not an old man yet, but I feel old." Their lives seemed to be measured by the pieces washed and ironed.

> *One piece, two pieces, three pieces,*
> *The clothes must be washed cleanly,*
> *Four pieces, five pieces, six pieces,*
> *The clothes must be ironed smoothly. . . .*
> *You say laundry is really cheap work;*
> *And only the Chinamen are willing to be so low. . . .*

Really, I, too, don't believe there is a future in it,
Washing people's sweat with your own blood
    and sweat.
Would you do that? Wouldn't you do that?
Year after year, with a nostalgic drop of tear;
Deep at night, by the flickering laundry light.

Working and living in their small shops located in white neighborhoods, the laundrymen felt caged. "Nobody can imagine such a life as ours in the 'Golden Mountain,'" a laundryman lamented in frustration. "I have been confined in this room for more than two years. Sometimes I feel so

A Chinese garment worker in San Francisco in the 1880s. Immigrant labor helped make the garment industry into one of the city's most important businesses. A century later, many Chinese immigrants continue to find work in garment factories.

lonesome in this small jail, I just want to go back to China."
Many of them led lives of quiet resignation, working to earn
enough money for a place to sleep and something to eat and
taking life as it was. One of them sadly said, "I can't expect a
life better than this and it is no use to try."

Their loneliness was made worse by the lack of Chinese women. After the destruction of records in the San
Francisco earthquake opened the door to America for a new
flurry of Chinese immigrants, more women began coming to
the United States from China. But Chinese men still greatly
outnumbered women. In 1930, 80% of the Chinese population was male.

But perhaps, some laundrymen thought, the hardships
and isolation they experienced in America would be only
temporary, a stepping-stone to a better life back in China. Said
one man, "I have no other hope but to get my money and get
back to China. What is the use of staying here; you can't be
an American here. We Chinese are not even allowed to become
citizens. If we were allowed, that might be a different story.
In that case, I think many of us Chinese would not think so
much of going back to China."

Not permitted to make America their home, laundrymen daydreamed about the land they had left. Their goal was
to return to their native villages with wealth and distinction.
In their imaginations, they saw themselves going home with
presents—perfumed soap (they called it "Golden Mountain
fragrance"), a sewing machine, and even a radio for their wives.
They would be admired by the villagers. They would swagger
down the village streets and show off by speaking to each
other in English. They would describe their laundries, and

they would build fine homes and sponsor "big affairs" such as the weddings of their children.

But most laundrymen did not make it back to China. Instead they became *Lo Wah Kiu*—old overseas Chinese who had stayed in America too long and had little chance of returning home. "We Chinese who are in this country are like convicts serving a term," protested a laundryman who had been in the United States for more than 20 years. Some tried to shorten their stay by gambling. "Once I saved about fifteen hundred dollars with which I planned to open a chop suey house," said a laundryman sorrowfully. "My partner-to-be didn't agree with me on some matter of the planning. I was disappointed. Seeing I had not enough to do it alone, I brought the money down to Chinatown and gambled with it. I thought if I could win about three more thousands, I would go back to China instead of opening a restaurant. I kept on gambling until I lost everything, within two weeks."

The Chinese laundrymen did not limit themselves to fantasies and complaints, however. They also engaged in politics and acts of resistance, claiming their rights as members of their adopted society. In New York during the 1930s, for example, large laundries owned by whites introduced washing machines and steam presses to cut costs. Lacking the money needed to buy similar equipment, the Chinese laundries offered lower prices and extra services, such as free mending and pickup and delivery. The white laundry operators responded by forming a citywide trade organization and setting minimum prices for laundry work. When they failed to force their Chinese competitors to raise their rates, the white laundry operators called for a boycott of Chinese

A professional letter writer has set up shop outside a Chinatown grocery. Such scribes wrote letters home to China for immigrants who could not read or write.

laundries, urging people to stop using the services of the Chinese.

In 1933, the white laundry organization went even further. It persuaded a city board to pass a law that required laundry operators to pay a $25 registration fee each year. Even worse, one-person laundries had to pay $1,000 as a bond, or deposit, to apply for a license. The law was clearly intended to drive small Chinese operators out of the laundry business.

Anxious and angry, hundreds of Chinese laundrymen protested against the new law. They attended a mass meeting sponsored by the Chinese Consolidated Benevolent Association (CCBA). But they quickly saw that the CCBA was more interested in collecting dues from the laundry workers than in fighting for their rights. So some of the laundrymen organized an independent laundry association called the Chinese Hand Laundry Alliance (CHLA). More than 2,400 people joined the CHLA, whose purpose was to unite Chinese laundrymen in a collective effort to protect their interests. The CHLA hired two lawyers and challenged the law. Arguing that the law unfairly discriminated against small laundries, the CHLA pressured city officials into lowering the bond fee to only $100.

New York City's Chinese laundrymen had discovered that they could enforce their rights and improve their lives by working together. They had proved that they could survive in a world that was mostly white, and that they could resist pressure from white competitors. But the Chinese in America remained separate and apart from the mainstream of American society.

A crowded tenement in San Francisco's Chinatown, 1888. Tourism created an image of a picturesque Chinatown, but the reality was grimmer. Many of the district's residents lived in overcrowded, substandard housing.

Chapter Four

The Growth of Chinatowns

THE CHINESE LAUNDRIES WERE ONLY PART OF THE world of Chinese America. Although many of the laundries were isolated in white neighborhoods, like tiny ethnic islands in a sea of whiteness, they were connected to the Chinatowns in American cities. These Chinatowns were larger ethnic islands, cradles of Chinese American culture. Together, they made up a Chinese "colony" in America.

By 1920, Chinatowns had formed in Los Angeles, Oakland, Chicago, Seattle, Portland, Sacramento, and Boston. But the biggest Chinatowns were in San Francisco and New York City; 40% of all Chinese people in America lived in those two cities. These big-city Chinatowns were different from the Chinatowns of the 19th century. The early Chinatowns had been way stations. Immigrant men passed through them on their way to the gold fields, farms, and railroads. In the 20th century, however, the Chinatowns developed into residential communities for families, Chinese economic centers, and tourist attractions.

Chinatown offered little luxury to its residents. In the 19th century, San Francisco's Chinatown was crammed with "bachelors." An investigation in 1885 had found that there were 14,550 bunks for single men in 10 blocks of Chinatown. After 1900, as more and more families occupied one-room dwellings in Chinatown, the overcrowding became even more severe. But Chinese were unable to buy or rent dwellings outside the Chinatowns. "A Chinaman cannot secure a residence outside of Chinatown, in San Francisco, no matter how much he may offer for it," a Chinese newspaper editor reported. "I endeavored to obtain a home nearer my newspaper office in San Francisco but found it utterly impossible and have always been compelled to live in the Chinese quarters."

Esther Wong, a student at Mills College, wrote in 1924, "Only a very few Chinese could find houses in American districts, for most house owners do not want Chinese tenants. They are forced to live in close quarters. The buildings are . . . dark and gloomy, with no bathrooms and no privacy." In Chinatown, a single man seldom had a room to himself. One immigrant recalled that in 1913, all of his cousins from his home village in China had shared a room in Chinatown. They slept, cooked, and ate in that one room. During the 1930s, when the United States plunged into a severe and long-lasting economic depression, Chinatown grew

Unmarried men in Chinatown lived in extremely cramped quarters. Privacy was rare; rooms were generally shared by two or more men.

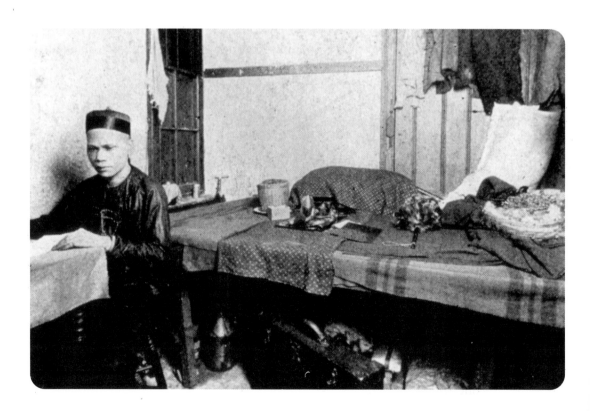

even more crowded as unemployed and needy Chinese people from rural areas came to San Francisco seeking relief.

Family quarters were not much more spacious than "bachelor" dwellings. In 1934, 276 families in Chinatown had 70 bathrooms and 114 kitchens among them. Six years later, 15,000 Chinese people lived in a confined area only five blocks by four blocks. Their rooms and tiny apartments were wedged between, above, and below shops, restaurants, and stores. More than three-quarters of these residences had no heating. Some of them had been built to house single men after the great earthquake and fire. They consisted of "tiny windowless rooms with hall toilets and kitchens and often no bath facilities anywhere." These bare dwellings now housed families. More than four-fifths of the dwellings in Chinatown failed to meet San Francisco's basic housing standards, compared with only one-fifth for the rest of the city. The tuberculosis rate in Chinatown was three times higher than in the rest of the city. Children were forced to play in the streets, for Chinatown had no parks.

Chinatown was a slum, a ghetto. It reinforced white stereotypes of the Chinese as unhealthy and undesirable immigrants who could not fit into American society. But this same image of the Chinese as aliens living in unsavory surroundings led to a new industry in Chinatown: tourism. To whites, Chinatown was a quaint and mysterious section of the city, a "foreign colony" in America. Advertisements promised that white tourists visiting Chinatown would experience the "sounds, the sights, and the smells of Canton." They could imagine themselves in "some hoary Mongolian city in the distant land of Cathay." They could "wander in the midst of the Orient" while still in the United States, and there they would see throngs of people with "strange faces" in the streets or sitting in restaurants eating "chop suey."

Behind the glitter of Chinatown's exotic image was the reality of dollars and cents. Tourism brought money into Chinatown. The importance of tourist profits was clear as early as 1900, when rumors spoke of an outbreak of bubonic plague in Chinatown. The Chinese Merchants' Association quickly made plans to hold a festival and reassured frightened tourists that they would not catch the plague in Chinatown.

After the 1906 earthquake, Chinatown had to be completely rebuilt. Many Chinese merchants worried when they saw that the first new structures were ordinary, cream-colored buildings, with nothing distinctive about them. The merchants wanted the rebuilt Chinatown to have an "Oriental atmosphere," so they were pleased that the new telephone company building resembled a Chinese temple.

The Chinese Six Companies, the largest and most important business association in Chinatown, saw that tourism could be very profitable. The association started a campaign to promote tourism. In 1909, it published a guidebook called *San Francisco's Chinatown.* This book gave tourists information about the community and assured them that they would be safe: "Visitors in Chinatown need fear no harm from members of the Chinese race."

Newspapers and magazines outside Chinatown joined the campaign. In 1917, the *San Francisco Chronicle* published a series of articles on "Historic Chinatown." One of these articles predicted that the "Oriental Quarter" with its "exotic atmosphere" was on the verge of a burst of economic growth. Thanks to the great fire of 1906, the newspaper stated, Chinatown had been rebuilt. It was now "thoroughly modern"

while still keeping its "Oriental charm and attractiveness." The author of the article insisted that Chinatown was perfectly safe, saying, "Some persons, those not familiar with the district, have the mistaken idea that when one enters Chinatown, particularly at night, one is in imminent danger of losing either one's life or one's purse." These fears were unfounded, for the "Oriental colony" was well policed and the Chinese people were "honest and law-abiding," glad to be visited by their "American neighbors."

Tourists were also told that they could comfortably eat Chinese food. The *Chronicle* informed its readers encouragingly that they need not worry about being baffled by unfamiliar food, for Chinese restaurant owners would help them choose a meal. The tourist industry even introduced a new dessert—the Chinese fortune cookie. Traditional Chinese meals do not include sweets, but white tourists expected some sort of dessert in Chinese restaurants. So a worker in the Kay Heong Noodle Factory invented a cookie that contained a small slip of paper with a Chinese proverb.

The San Francisco Chamber of Commerce, a business association, played a leading part in making Chinatown a

The growth of Chinatowns created more jobs in the Chinese ethnic economy. Restaurants employed immigrants as cooks and waiters.

tourist attraction, knowing that tourists who came to see Chinatown would spend money throughout the city. The Chamber of Commerce published full-page ads describing the "exotic beauty" of the "Chinese colony." The Grayline Bus Company also helped boost the Chinatown tourist trade, and in 1935, the bus company proudly announced that it had introduced more than 10,000 tourists to Chinatown that year.

In 1938, Chinatown merchants formed a new organization to increase the flow of tourist dollars into San Francisco and Chinatown. They recommended that dingy back alleys be turned into picturesque little lanes. They also wanted to increase the amount of Chinese architecture and decoration in Chinatown, and to revive traditional Chinese festivals and celebrations. The Chinese New Year, celebrated in February with parades, was an especially good "tourist catcher."

Tourist dollars came pouring in. San Francisco made $28 million from tourism in 1938; nearly one-fifth of this amount was spent in Chinatown. An editorial in the *Chinese Digest* announced that Chinatown had become the city's second most popular spot, next to Golden Gate Park.

Tourism helped the Chinese in America survive after the labor unions and racial discrimination had forced Chinese workers out of the general labor market. But, during the Great Depression of the 1930s, Chinese suffered from severe unemployment. Thousands of jobless Chinese people needed welfare money; in 1931, almost one-sixth of the Chinese population of San Francisco received welfare aid from the state.

In this time of economic hardship, tourism offered jobs and hope. The editor of the *Chinese Digest* pointed out in 1935 that the tourist trade had become Chinatown's main

source of income. He urged the community to do everything
it could to protect its "golden goose," and he asked, "Where
will our bazaars be within a few years, if no visitors come to
Chinatown? Where will our fancy chop suey neon signs end
up? . . . Where can the younger generation turn to, to find any
employment outside of Chinatown?" Tourism had become
necessary, and the strategy for Chinatown was clear: "Make
tourists WANT to come; and when they come, let us have
something to SHOW them!"

Tourists were shown a fantasy land, a strange place
they had read about in stories and novels, or had seen in
Hollywood movies about Fu Manchu and Charlie Chan.
Guided through the narrow alleys of this "wicked Orient,"
tourists were warned by white guides to stick together and not
stray from the group, or else a hatchet man might get them.
The visitors peered into the dark shadows of dim alleys. In
the streets and buildings they saw mysterious and sometimes

*In the early days,
Chinatown was
overwhelmingly a
community of men.*

A tourist has her palm read in a Chinese shop. Fortune-telling, imported artifacts, and other "exotic" features drew visitors to Chinatown, which soon became one of San Francisco's leading tourist attractions.

sinister-looking Chinese characters—who had been hired by the guides to provide local color.

"You read about underground tunnels in old China-town?" Gim Chang, who had grown up in Chinatown and operated a business there for decades, asked an interviewer in the 1970s. "I know nothing about them. I'm quite sure they didn't exist at all." But the tourist business created and exploited the image of Chinatown as a sinful and dangerous place. "Much to the opposition of the respectable Chinese," a Chinese American woman said in 1920, "the horrors and vices of the San Francisco's Chinatown were heralded to the world."

Chinese children resented the tourist invasions and the lies told about Chinatown to the visitors. They would follow the tours and shout "liar" at the guides. "Many of the guides created false impressions in the minds of tourists, concerning Chinese habits and life," complained Esther Wong in 1924. Once a tourist wandered into the Chinese YWCA and asked "in broken English for the location of the underground dungeons and opium dens." Told that no such places existed, he "was quite disappointed and Chinatown lost its glamour to him."

San Francisco had the largest Chinatown in America, but the second largest was in New York City. In 1907, a magazine writer described the birth of New York's China-town: "The Chinatown began with the establishment some thirty-five years ago of the Wo Kee Company's tea store in Mott Street. At that time a Chinaman was a sight to be stared at in the streets of New York." The city's Chinese population grew from 120 in 1870 to 2,600 in 1890, and a Chinese face was no longer a rare sight. As Chinese newcomers gathered in

New York, they expanded their colony to Doyers, Pell, Bayard, and Canal streets, moving into buildings once inhabited by Irish and German families.

In the 20th century, the Chinese population of New York rose rapidly. It increased from 4,614 in 1910 to 12,753 in 1940. Half of the Chinese residents lived in Chinatown, and many of them were men. In New York's Chinatown, there were six men to every woman, compared with only two men to every woman in San Francisco's Chinatown. There were fewer families in New York's Chinatown, which was mainly a community of men living in crowded, small rooms and apartments. New York's Chinatown also contained a greater share of immigrants than San Francisco's Chinatown. Less than one-third of the Chinese people in New York City in 1940 had been born in America, while almost two-thirds of San Francisco's Chinese population was American-born. Still largely composed of "bachelors" and immigrants, New York's Chinatown had not moved as far as San Francisco's Chinatown toward a settled family society. But New York's Chinatown was a tourist attraction. The early Chinese inhabitants of New York worked mostly in cigar factories, and the grocery stores, herb shops, barbershops, and restaurants of Chinatown served Chinese customers. During the 1890s, Chinatown began to attract white tourists. These tourists read in a guidebook to the city: "Mott, Pell and Doyers streets and vicinity are now given over to the Chinese. . . . The district is a veritable 'Chinatown' with all the filth, immorality, and picturesque foreignness which that name implies."

In the early 20th century, the tourist trade in New York's Chinatown became a booming business. A white man who called himself the "mayor of Chinatown" guided tourists around the district, which he called his "reservation." He and his thuggish guides lured visitors into their tours, saying that they would escort tourists safely through the menacing dark alleys. As in San Francisco, the guides hired Chinese to put on shows for their guests. Soon bus companies entered the tourist trade, conducting tours through the curved, narrow streets of Chinatown past curio shops, stores, and restaurants. As the gawking tourists rode by in sight-seeing buses, they listened to wild stories of this exotic place.

The tourist trade was filled with contradictions. On one hand, tourists were shown filthy alleys and told wild stories about the Chinese. On the other, they were encouraged to dine in Chinatown and assured that they need not worry about unsanitary conditions. "A visit to Chinatown," the *New York City Guide* of 1939 recommended, "should include dinner at one of the numerous restaurants declared by the Board of Health to be among the cleanest in the city."

Chinatowns in San Francisco and New York and across the country were cultural islands, cut off from the mainstream of American society. White Americans viewed Chinatowns as alien places in the heart of America, places to visit as tourists. By the 1930s, many of the more sensational and false practices of the tourist trade had disappeared. But still the economy of the Chinatowns depended largely on providing services, including tourist services. "Wherever the Chinese are," said one observer in 1942, "it has been possible to count the variations in the ways they can earn their living on the fingers of the hand—chop suey and chow mein restaurants, Chinese art and gift shops, native grocery stores that sell foodstuffs imported from China to the local Chinese community and Chinese laundries."

Most Chinese American businesses were fairly small, but one of them did become a huge financial success. While it was not dependent on tourism and not located in Chinatown, Joe Shoong's enterprise was connected to Chinatown because it drew upon Chinatown for its labor supply. In 1903, Shoong opened the China Toggery dry-goods store in Vallejo, California. After the 1906 earthquake, he moved his store to San Francisco. The business did well, and Shoong added branch stores in California, Oregon, and Washington. In 1928, with 16 stores, he renamed his enterprise the National Dollar Stores. "Do you know why they call it the National Dollar Store?" said Kenneth Lim, a manager for more than 30 years. "In the beginning they sold the goods for nothing over a dollar. That's how they started out. . . . Clothing, everything, was under one dollar."

Lim described the early and exciting success of the store: "It's just crowded like anything, because they sold at a pretty low margin. Sometimes, even if it was just a little over a dollar, they sold it for a dollar, and when we had that kind of a sale (famous quality sheets), we used to open up a box, with so many hundred sheets. We collect the money and ring it up, so it was fast. Oh, everything was really fast."

Shoong's stores had Chinese managers, but the workers who dealt with the public were white, and so were most of the customers. Behind the scenes, however, the workers in stockrooms and factories were Chinese. In fact, Shoong's business relied heavily on the exploitation of Chinese labor. For example, the women's dresses sold in the National Dollar Stores were made by low-paid Chinese garment workers in San Francisco's Chinatown. In 1937, these seamstresses organized themselves into the Chinese Ladies Garment Workers

and went on strike against the garment factory owned by National Dollar. The strike lasted 13 weeks, the longest in Chinatown's history, but the workers lost when their employer closed the factory rather than yield to their demands. Shoong could simply open a new factory elsewhere, for his success had made him very wealthy. By then he owned 37 stores and had been described by *Time* magazine as "the richest, best-known Chinese businessman in the U.S."

But Shoong and a few other wealthy Chinese businessmen were exceptional. The huge majority of Chinese were trapped in Chinatowns and in dead-end jobs. According to the 1940 United States Census, 61% of all the Chinese in the labor force were manual laborers. Almost all of them worked in laundries, garment factories, and restaurants. Even those Chinese who were U.S. citizens and had been educated in the

United States did not do much better—59% of them were manual laborers.

Viewed from within, Chinatown was not a quaint and colorful tourist attraction. For the people living there, it was their home and community—a place where they could live "a warmer, freer, and more human life among their relatives and friends than among strangers." The grocery stores stocked familiar foods such as Chinese cabbage, dried mushrooms, salted fish, canned lichees, soy sauce, sea cucumber, bamboo shoots, shark fins, dried boned ducks' feet, salted duck eggs, bean sprouts, and Chinese roast duck. The clothing stores sold pants and shoes that fit the Chinese. In Chinatown, they could find newspapers in Chinese, herb shops, Chinese theaters, and barbershops where they could have their hair cut and arranged in the proper styles. Chinatown restaurants served "bachelors" cheap but tasty food; they also offered lavish nine-course dinners to wealthy Chinese families, especially on Sundays.

Chinatown also had temples, Chinese language schools, and centers for family and community associations. Some of the stores served as post offices; said one resident, "Folks in Canton usually wrote to their relatives in the United States in care of these stores." When visiting the outside world, among whites, Chinese felt they had to be reserved and silent. But among themselves in Chinatown they could untie their tongues, for they liked to "talk, and talk loudly." To its inhabitants, Chinatown was "a home away from home, where the Chinese felt at ease and the Americans became the foreigners." Inside Chinatown, the Chinese immigrants could tell jokes and laugh among themselves. They could hear folk tales from the homeland told and retold, and they could pretend that Chinatown was "really China."

Facing a new future in the United States, a young immigrant waits to be released with his family from Angel Island.

Chapter Five

The Children of Chinatown

OVER THE YEARS, CHINATOWN BECAME A PLACE WHERE children lived. The immigration of Chinese women after the 1906 San Francisco earthquake meant that families could form in the Chinese community. It had not always been that way.

In 1900, nine-tenths of the Chinese people in the United States had been born in China. Most of them were men. Children were rare—only 3.5% of the Chinese were under 15 years of age, compared with 35% for the total American population. "The greatest impression I have of my childhood in those days was that at that time there were very few families in Chinatown," recalled a resident. "Babies were looked on with a kind of wonder."

But in the 20th century, as Chinese women began arriving in the United States, the number of American-born Chinese grew quickly. By 1940, 52% of the Chinese in America had been born in the United States. Communities that had once been "bachelor" societies had become centers of family life.

To make space for their children, parents tore down the walls of rooms and turned single men's quarters into apartments for families. "Our room was designed for the old 'bachelors' who used to come over here," said a second-generation Chinese American. "All my father did was break down some of the walls and we lived there over the store." As a child growing up in San Francisco's Chinatown, Frank Eng lived with his parents and seven siblings in one big room attached to the family store. He described their home: "What they did, you see, was divide the whole room. There was a high ceiling and they just built another floor between the ceiling and the regular floor, and we lived on top."

A Chinese American woman recalled that her family lived in their garment factory. "When we lived on Clay Street in San Francisco my father rented a store there," she said. "The front was the factory, the back was where we lived. . . . And my father had the long cutting table. We slept there too. Daytime it was a cutting table, nighttime it was our bed."

In their Chinatown world, children watched their parents at work—laundrymen expertly wielding hot irons, seamstresses operating sewing machines in noisy garment factories, and cooks chopping carrots and celery in cramped restaurant kitchens. The youngsters saw that their parents had to work long hours. Said one, "My father would get up and leave the house about six in the morning and not close the store until almost nine at night. So what's that? Fifteen hours?" The children worked, too: "If your parents had a business definitely you're going to stay around to help. You don't even demand to be paid because it's your duty to do so."

After school each day, the children did their share of work, peeling shrimp and cutting onions in the alley behind the family restaurant, or loading dirty clothes into the washing machines of the family laundry. "I began by helping my parents fold towels and handkerchiefs, very simple things," one of them said years later. "When I got to be eight or nine years old they showed me how to work the presses and I went from T-shirts and handkerchiefs to complicated things like shirts."

Younger children went with their mothers to the factory. "My mother tied me to her back and sewed," recalled a man who was a child in San Francisco's Chinatown during the 1930s. He listed his memories of those early days: "The constant drum of sewing machines. The chatter of Cantonese.

The F car rolling and rumbling from somewhere through Stockton Street near the tunnel. Stop; screeching and ding-ding off again to somewhere not Chinatown."

That "somewhere not Chinatown," the children discovered, could be very unfriendly. "In those days, the boundaries were from Kearny to Powell, and from California to Broadway," an old-timer remembered, naming the streets that bordered San Francisco's Chinatown. "If you ever passed them and went out there, the white kids would throw stones at you." Chinese parents repeatedly warned their children about "the whites out there," the "foreign devils," the "western people": "Don't go too far because the white people are

In the early 20th century, a new sight appeared in Chinatown: children. The arrival of Chinese women meant that families could form and a Chinese American community could grow.

against you," parents would say. "They may throw a rock or do something to hurt you."

By the time the Chinese second generation was forming, immigration from Japan was under way, and young Chinese Americans were sometimes called "Japs." Occasionally they snapped back, "How do you know we're Japs?" More often, however, they were insulted with the names "Chinks" and "Chinamen."

During the 1920s, a Chinese college student from Hawaii was distressed to find that the Chinese were treated very differently in California than in Hawaii. In Hawaii, she had grown up in a world where the majority of the people looked like her. She was used to a "friendly, democratic, cosmopolitan spirit and atmosphere." She saw herself as an American, a citizen by birth. "I did not stop to think of myself as being distinctly a Chinese and of my friends as being distinctly Americans, or Japanese, or some other nationality," she wrote. "It never occurred to me that I am only a Chinese-made American in spirit."

When she arrived in Los Angeles, she was thrilled to be on the mainland. But when she went to the university to register, she noticed people staring at her as though she were "a strange being." A disturbing discovery awaited her. "I realized very soon that I was not an American in spite of the fact that I had citizenship privileges," she recounted. "At the University, I was referred to as a FOREIGN STUDENT. I objected to being called such at first; I insisted that I was an American. . . . But soon I learned that was laughed at. . . ."

Mocked by whites, the young woman was "disappointed and deeply hurt" by their stares and sneers. She learned painfully that she was "a foreigner—a Chinese."

Lonely and homesick for Hawaii, she felt humiliated to think that she had been proud of her American citizenship when in reality her citizenship meant "nothing—nothing in the United States." By the "United States," she was referring to the American mainland, where the Chinese had been forced to retreat into ethnic islands. In Hawaii, the Chinese were part of the general society, but on the mainland they lived in their own separate economic and cultural colonies.

Chinese parents on the mainland tried to prepare their children for the anti-Chinese prejudice they would experience. "Be proud that you're Chinese," they told their children. "Yes, legally you are Americans, but you will not be accepted. Look at your face—it is Chinese. But don't worry, just show them how smart you are because you have a superior heritage."

The Chinese Primary School on Clay Street in San Francisco's Chinatown, around 1910. Chinese children were not allowed to enter regular public schools until the late 1920s.

Another parent urged, "Don't pay any attention to the names the white children call you. They're just barbarians! Just be as nice as possible to them, because you have a superior culture."

Still, the racial slurs stung and the rejection hurt. One Chinese American woman recalled insults from white children. "They yelled these obscenities to us each time we would be approaching the school," she said. "'Ching Chong Chinamen sitting on a rail,' and oh, funny sounds, like 'eeyauyau-yauyau!'—things like that." Another woman remembered how she was called a "Chink" and "resented it bitterly." A man said that he had never been near whites until he entered junior high school. There they made him feel uncomfortable, like an outsider. A Chinese American high-school student told an interviewer in 1924 that his fellow students talked rudely to him and claimed he was not a citizen. He added proudly, "Even though their words hurt me I have never been ashamed of being a Chinese and never have I wished I were a white man."

One Chinese youth who was called "Chink" by the white students said, "It didn't anger me. I just thought, well, there are people in this world who are ignorant, so why get into a fight?" But other Chinese boys saw it differently. "When someone would call me 'Chink,'" one of them snarled, "I didn't like that. So, big or small, I didn't care what you were, I'd straighten that up right now." Once during a study period in high school, he was approached by a white student who wanted to know how to work on a problem. The white boy said, "Hey, Chink, how do you do this?" The Chinese boy promptly gave him an answer with his fist. The teacher came over and asked what had happened, and the Chinese boy replied: "Well, he wanted some help with a problem and I'm showing him the chinky way of doing it."

Children were often told by their parents to ignore the abuse and concentrate instead on their studies. The immigrant generation hoped that their children would help the Chinese in America gain dignity. "Our parents *used* the children to vent their frustration on, trying to get us all to *get ahead*," a second-generation Chinese American man explained. "And there was a lot of frustration inside of Chinatown, too, because the Chinese felt themselves to be such noble creatures,

Although they wear Western clothing, several of these Chinese boys have not yet gotten American-style haircuts. American and Chinese influences were mixed in the lives of many youthful immigrants and second-generation Chinese Americans.

and yet they were subjugated, they were discriminated against, they couldn't leave the area, they couldn't buy houses, they couldn't get any kind of job."

Although they came from a "different shore" than the European immigrants and had been forced to be strangers in America, many Chinese immigrants began to feel a new closeness to the United States when they started families in their adopted country. "America is my new home because she has become my children's home," said a mother. "She is my country now because she is the mother country of my children."

A fourth-grade class in New York's Chinatown, 1961. The Chinese American community in New York became the second largest in the country, after San Francisco.

Through their children, the Chinese immigrants were becoming connected to America. Many of these hopeful parents sacrificed their own comfort and worked hard for the sake of their children. They wanted the children to have the opportunities and rights that they had been denied. They urged their children to study hard, hoping that education would protect the younger generation from racism; parents did not want to see their sons and daughters suffering as they had suffered, "eating bitterness." An immigrant father told his son, "I've worked my fingers to the bones for you boys to get yourself an education. If you cannot be better than they [the whites] are, try to be their equal anyway, because that way, one of these days, you can be up there too."

By the late 1960s, young Chinese Americans shared the styles, customs, and values of mainstream society—a fact that sometimes perplexed and distressed their elderly, more traditional relatives.

73

Unable to fit into the roles prepared for her by Chinese family tradition or prejudice in the American workplace, Jade Snow Wong created her own identity as a potter and writer. This picture was taken in 1952, when she was thirty years old.

Chapter Six

Between Two Worlds

FOR THE SECOND-GENERATION CHINESE IN AMERICA, education was seen as the way to get out of the Chinatown ghetto. In the old country, peasants were too poor to send their children to school, but in the United States the immigrants could enroll their children in public school. One girl's parents told her, "Think of all the marvelous things you can learn here. You can get one of the best educations here. This is a wonderful country."

The children of Chinatown went to public schools where they said the pledge of allegiance to the flag of the United States and learned about American culture. They came under the influence of their teachers. A Chinese man in San Francisco remembered how a teacher named Mr. Weinstein first gave him the idea of citizenship, and how Miss Davis and Mrs. Beck brought him "closer to American ideals and American patriotism." But a conflict arose within the hearts of these children as they found themselves pulled between two worlds.

To be American, it seemed, was to lose their Chinese identity. "In the English school they didn't believe in Chinese customs," said a former student. The teachers tried to "dissuade us from speaking Cantonese; they tried to dissuade us from everything Chinese. Their view of the Chinese ways was that they were evil, heathen, non-Christian." One of this boy's teachers scolded him, "If you're gonna be an American, ya might as well learn ta speak English."

But to their parents, these children were also Chinese. They had to learn the Chinese language and the culture of the old country. So after attending American school all day, they went to Chinese school. One second-generation man described his Chinese education: "My Chinese school career began when I was five years old. The school was on Grant

Ave. We went to Chinese school immediately after American school which was about 4 or 5 P.M. and stayed there till about 7 or 8 P.M." They also had classes at Chinese school on Saturday mornings. At the Chinese school, young people studied Chinese language, history, literature, and philosophy.

Many of the children thought Chinese school was a burden. They did not always take their Chinese studies seriously. A second-generation Chinese American woman described the students this way: "In the American schools they are anxious to get ahead of their classmates, while their attitude toward the Chinese learning is indifferent. Consequently, the only language which the majority of the Chinese Americans can read and write is English." Thomas W. Chinn, who founded the *Chinese Digest* in 1935, grew up in San Francisco's Chinatown in the 1920s and went to Chinese school. "Somehow," he said, "we never became proficient in reading or writing Chinese—probably because we never thought of ourselves as needing Chinese. After all, weren't we Americans?"

The second-generation Chinese moved between two cultures. Their schools were American, but at home the Chinese and American worlds met. Sometimes these two worlds clashed. As they grew up, many second-generation Chinese saw America as their permanent home and China as remote and foreign. Many changed their Chinese first names to American ones: from Soo Fei to Fay, Wei Lim to William, Teong to Ted, Mei Guen to Mae Gwen, Yim Jun to Jean, Yim Sunn to Shelley, and Yoon to June. They also wanted to look American. A woman who worked for the Congregational Mission in San Francisco's Chinatown for 27 years described the Chinese youth in 1924: "The Chinese girls bob their hair, wear sleeveless dresses, and look just like the little American flappers."

Chinese teenagers mixed the two cultures every day without thinking much about it. Said one, "On weekends we'd go eat *wonton* (a Chinese soup) and drink orange freeze at the soda fountain." Many youngsters saw themselves as modern and their parents as old-fashioned. "My parents wanted me to grow up a good Chinese girl, but I am an American and I can't accept all the old Chinese ways and ideas," explained Flora Belle Jan of Fresno, California, in 1924. "A few years ago when my Mother took me to worship at the shrine of my ancestor and offer a plate of food, I decided it was time to stop this foolish custom. So I got up and slammed down the rice in front of the idol and said, 'So long Old Top, I don't believe in you anyway.'"

Sometimes the break from their parents and from Chinese roots meant that young Chinese people also rejected aspects of their own identities. "When I was young, before thirteen," admitted one woman, "I used to wish I had light hair and blue eyes." An American-born Chinese writer reported in the *Chinese Digest* in 1939 that second-generation Chinese girls were as American as "pink lemonade in a Kansas fair." He added, "If you were to close your eyes for a moment, you'd be certain they were *real* Americans."

These modern, Americanized second-generation Chinese were sometimes given mocking nicknames by the older folk of the immigrant generation. They were called *t'oa jee doy* ("one who is ignorant of Chinese culture") and *chok sing* ("bamboo pole," meaning "empty inside like the bamboo").

Many American-born Chinese, especially the more educated youngsters, simply wanted more independence and

78

more choice for themselves than their parents allowed. Chinese girls found they had to challenge traditional Chinese attitudes toward women. "My parents do not believe in freedom of women and children," asserted one of them. "I believe in complete freedom of women. A woman should be responsible to no one but herself." The daughter of a Chinese laundryman in Baltimore broke away from her father's expectations. "My father did not want me to go on to college at all," she said. "He thought girls shouldn't have an education. He wanted me to get married, he wanted to match me with all sorts of men. And I didn't want to do that. I wanted to go to school. And he said, 'If you want to go to school and you disobey me, I'll disown you.' And I said, 'Well, I'll just have to leave. Good-bye, papa.'"

For the second-generation Chinese women, independence meant the freedom to choose their own husbands, to marry because of love rather than family arrangements. When Naomi Jung turned 18, she resisted her father's efforts to find a husband for her through a matchmaker in the traditional Chinese way. "Don't worry about me," she bluntly told him. Another woman, a student at Stanford University, told an interviewer in 1924, "My parents wanted to hold to the idea of selecting a husband for me, but I would not accept their choices. . . . We younger Chinese make fun of the old Chinese idea according to which the parents made all arrangements for the marriage of their children."

But in reality, the choice—to be Chinese or to be American—was not so clear-cut. The second generation of Chinese people in America could not completely belong to either world. Wrote one, "With their American ideas, thoughts, attitudes, and customs, they cannot feel at home with the Chinese people though they have a Chinese appearance. Because of their physical appearance, they are denied the opportunities to achieve the better social and economic status which they desire in the American community."

Many second-generation Chinese men and women were confused and troubled by the feeling of being torn between two worlds. One man commented, "There was endless discussion about what to do about the dilemma of being *caught in between* . . . being loyal to the parents and their ways and yet trying to assess the good from both sides. We used to call ourselves just a 'marginal man,' caught between two cultures."

They felt the pushes and pulls of two worlds—the Chinese and the American. "I think that both sides are pulling equally—one the land of freedom which was my birthplace, my home—the other, my parents' home, my race's abode and my motherland," a second-generation man explained thoughtfully. "To me they both hold the same attraction but sometimes America seems to get me more over China and I say that if any place shall be my home in the old age it *shall* be America. Now in regard to Americans—I love them just as well as my own race but they don't give us the same respect (this is just some, not all). They spite us, they hate us and they wish we were never in America." Many of the children of Chinatown grew up feeling isolated and cut off, like islands between two cultural continents, unsure of where they belonged.

For second-generation Chinese Americans, the tension between two identities was sometimes hard to bear. This was especially true for Chinese American daughters. One who felt this tension was Jade Snow Wong, who described her experiences in her autobiography, *Fifth Chinese Daughter.*

Jade Snow Wong was not a typical second-generation Chinese American, for her father was a businessman and a Christian. Still, she experienced many of the problems of being caught between two worlds. For her, growing up and coming of age in America, where she was born, was a complicated business. She found herself searching for a bridge from Chinatown to the larger society, looking for an identity that would allow her to be both Chinese and American.

As a child, Jade Snow lived in San Francisco's Chinatown, a community separated from the "outside foreign American world." Her father ran a garment factory, and her family lived in an apartment behind the business. Her father, the son of a merchant, had come to San Francisco with his wife in the first decade of the 20th century. Jade Snow's mother had been raised according to Chinese custom. Her feet had been bound when she was a small child so that they would remain tiny and deformed, a feature that was considered beautiful in traditional Chinese culture. Jade Snow recalled that her mother had "little, two-and-a-half inch, bound feet," and that her father called his wife "my inferior woman." Her father taught Jade Snow her first lessons from Chinese books, and her mother made her bright silk Chinese dresses for holidays such as Chinese New Year's Day, when she would sit on her father's shoulders to watch the festivities.

Jade Snow Wong (right, at age 11) found that growing up in Chinese America was a complicated business. She struggled to combine Chinese obedience with American freedom; she also fought racial and sexual stereotyping.

Jade Snow's father believed that all Chinese children in America should learn their ancestral language. One evening after dinner, he announced to eight-year-old Jade Snow and the rest of the family that the time had come for her to attend Chinese evening school. As his daughter, she was expected to know Chinese and to be familiar with China's great rivers, its poetry, and its culture. Jade Snow's Chinese identity was also reinforced by the family meals of rice and Chinese dishes.

When her brother was born, Jade Snow discovered what it meant to be a Chinese daughter. Her parents had had five daughters in a row, and the birth of a boy caused much celebration in the Wong family. The happy parents named the boy Forgiveness from Heaven because they had been afraid that Heaven had been punishing them by sending them only girls. Jade Snow overheard a conversation between two of her older sisters. "This joyfulness springs only from the fact that the child is at last a son," said one sister. She added that when a daughter was born, "the house was quiet."

As she lay in bed that night, Jade Snow tried to understand what she had heard. She realized then that Forgiveness from Heaven was more important to her parents because he was a boy. She was "unalterably less significant than the new son in their family."

The behavior of other family members soon confirmed what she had realized. When Uncle Bing came to visit the family, he congratulated her father on the birth of a son: "What a fine boy; what intelligent features! Here is a piece of money to buy some candy." Jade Snow watched Uncle Bing tuck a coin into the baby's hand, a traditional custom. As a boy, Forgiveness received special gifts from relatives and friends. He was also entitled to special support from his parents. They sent him to college, but required Jade Snow to pay for her own college education. Her father explained why he treated Forgiveness differently than his daughters. Sons, he told her, helped carry on a family's name and its heritage, and therefore they must have priority over daughters, who leave their parents to help carry on the heritage of their husbands' families.

But by this time, Jade Snow Wong was no longer a "dutiful" Chinese daughter. She thought it was unfair that her gender should determine her destiny, making her the carrier of "the heritage for other names." She had been told by her mother that she should not pursue a career. To have "a natural or complete life" as a woman she should be a wife and mother. "As you mature," her mother said, "you should have a husband to take care of you in sickness, and when you are older, your children should relieve your loneliness."

Jade Snow's mother wanted the girl's life to have a traditional Chinese meaning. To this Chinese mother, women were defined by their relationships with men. They had no existence apart from fathers and husbands and oldest sons. In the privacy of her bedroom, Jade Snow protested the unfairness of it all. "There are no ancestral pilgrimages to be made in the United States!" she cried. "I can't help being born a girl." She did not want to marry just to raise sons. "I am a person, besides being a female! Don't the Chinese admit that women also have feelings and minds?"

In fact, Jade Snow's father had cultivated a spirit of independence in her. He was Western in many ways. Shortly after his arrival in San Francisco, he had become a Christian. And he realized that America was a different world from China. He told his wife, "Do not bind our daughters' feet.

Here in America is an entirely different set of standards, which does not require that women sway helplessly on little feet to qualify them for good matches as well-born women who do not have to work. Here in Golden Mountain, the people, and even women, have individual dignity and rights of their own."

Jade Snow's father did not want her to know Chinese culture only. He also wanted her to have an American education, including training in Western music. He sent her to take piano lessons so she could play Beethoven, Chopin, and Mozart. "Education is your path to freedom," he told her. "In China, you would have had little private tutoring and no free advanced schooling. Make the most of your American opportunity."

Jade Snow followed her father's advice. But her American education only widened the gap between herself and Chinese culture. In elementary school, she learned new English-language games such as "Farmer in the Dell" and "London Bridge Is Falling Down." She also memorized a poem about Jack and Jill. In the fourth grade, she admired a teacher who had wavy blonde hair, fair skin, and blue eyes. One incident that Jade Snow would always remember occurred in the schoolyard. During a baseball game, she was accidentally hit on the hand by a carelessly flung bat. Hurt, she found herself held by her teacher who gently rubbed her sore hand and wiped away her tears. Cuddled by her teacher, she experienced a "very strange feeling." She could not remember when her mother had embraced her to give her comfort. From then on, Jade Snow was more and more aware of the difference between "'foreign' American ways" and "Chinese ways." And she realized uncomfortably that she could choose between the two.

Young Jade Snow moved back and forth between her American and Chinese cultures. She eagerly read the comic strips—"Bringing Up Father," "Dick Tracy," and "The Katzenjammer Kids"—and then she did her Chinese lessons. She went to the movie house to see films about cowboys and Tarzan, and she also attended plays at the Chinese theater. For a while she felt that she could live in both worlds. But she was to learn that there was a division between them. She encountered the barrier of racism.

At the beginning of seventh grade, Jade Snow enrolled in a junior high school outside her neighborhood because her father did not want her to study at a school where there were "tough" boys. She was the only Chinese student at the new school, and she felt shy about making friends with her "foreign" classmates. One day, after school, a boy named Richard approached her and shouted, "Chinky, Chinky, Chinaman." Then he threw an eraser at her. Dancing around her gleefully, he teased, "Look at the eraser mark on the yellow Chinaman. Chinky, Chinky, no tickee, no washee, no shirtee!"

Jade Snow dismissed Richard as ignorant. "Everybody knew," she thought to herself, "that the Chinese people had a superior culture." Her ancestors had made important inventions such as the compass, gunpowder, and paper. Still, she now realized that many white people would see her as a stranger because of her race.

In high school, Jade Snow decided that she wanted to go to college. She had no money, however, and her father was not willing to help her. So she did housework, cleaning and cooking for white families, hoping that her savings, together with a scholarship, would be enough for her to attend the University of California at Berkeley. But she failed to win a

Katherine Cheung, photographed in 1935, was typical of the new, nontraditional Chinese American woman. She became a pilot while still in high school.

scholarship. Her friend Joe encouraged her not to give up her dream of going to college, suggesting that she should enroll in San Francisco Junior College.

At the junior college, Jade Snow took Latin, chemistry, and sociology. The last course, taken just to meet a requirement, changed her world and her way of thinking. As she sat in class one day, she heard her professor make a startling statement. During a lecture on the history of the family in American society, he argued that parents could no longer demand unquestioning obedience from their children. Parents, he said, should recognize the individuality and rights of young people—an idea that seemed revolutionary to Jade Snow Wong.

Jade Snow applied this idea to her own life. She asked herself: "Could it be that Daddy and Mama, although they were living in San Francisco in the year 1938, actually had not left the Chinese world of thirty years ago? Could it be that they were forgetting that Jade Snow would soon become a woman in a new America, not a woman in old China?" Soon afterward, as Jade Snow was leaving her house for a date with a boy, her father stopped her and asked whether she had his permission to go out. "I can now think for myself," she answered, "and you and Mama should not demand unquestioning obedience from me." Insisting that she had rights of her own, she continued, "I am an individual besides being your fifth daughter." Her declaration of independence shocked her father. He demanded to know where she had learned such things and said, "Do not try to force foreign ideas into my home."

After Jade Snow graduated from junior college, she transferred to Mills College. She no longer tried to bring the new Western learning into her Chinese home. Instead, she simply lived two separate lives. When she visited her parents on weekends, she quietly performed the usual daughterly duties. Back at school during the week, she again became an individual with ideas and opinions of her own.

Yet this divided life was not satisfying. Jade Snow wanted recognition from her father. When he came to Mills College for her graduation ceremony in 1942, he visited the art gallery with his daughter. There he saw some pottery she had made in an art class. Impressed with her work, he asked, "Did you do these by yourself? You may not know this, but my father, your grandfather, was artistically inclined and very interested in handwork. . . . He would have been happy to see your work." Jade Snow knew that it would not have been becoming for a Chinese daughter to say "Thank you" for an indirect compliment, so she replied with the proper formula: "Is that so?" But she was happy. Finally she felt appreciated and accepted. She noticed, however, that her pottery was more meaningful to her father than her excellent grades. She did not realize at the time how much his remark would influence her choice of a career.

After graduating from college, Wong began looking for a job. One interviewer told her to look for jobs only in Chinese firms, warning her that racial prejudice would keep her from being hired or advancing in white companies.

Later, while working as a secretary for the navy, Wong decided she wanted to do something more interesting and important than answering the phone and typing letters. But she discovered she faced discrimination not only as a Chinese but also as a woman. When she asked her boss about the chance of getting a better job, he gave her "straight" advice.

*The growth of families created a housing crisis in San Francisco's
Chinatown, where parents and children were forced to squeeze into
tiny bachelor quarters.*

"Don't you know by now that as long as you are a woman," he said, "you can't compete for an equal salary in a man's world?"

Discouraged and depressed, Wong retreated to the Santa Cruz Mountains for a vacation. She had to think about who she was and wanted to be. One morning she rose early and hiked on a mountain trail. Sitting on a log in the shade of a bay tree, she thought about how she wanted to "silence the narrow thinking of all the 'Richards' and the 'placement officers.'" Suddenly she saw a new path opening before her. She would write about the Chinese experience, about herself. She *could* become a writer; as a writer, she would not be "competing against men." To earn a living, she would also sell her pottery. After Wong returned from the mountains, she wrote her autobiography. It was published by a major publishing company in 1945. She also opened her own ceramics shop in Chinatown.

Jade Snow Wong's father was impressed by his daughter's business success. He showed her a copy of a letter that he had written decades earlier. When he first came to America, he had been urged by his cousin to return to China. But he had replied, "You do not realize the shameful and degraded position into which the Chinese culture has pushed its women. Here in America, the Christian concept allows women their freedom and individuality. I wish my daughters to have this Christian opportunity." After reading this letter to Jade Snow, he said, "It is good to have you home again!"

Job opportunities were especially limited for women immigrants, who often found work only in crowded, unsafe garment sweatshops in the Chinatowns of New York and San Francisco.

JADE SNOW WONG MADE HER OWN PLACE IN THE world. But she had to invent a role for herself because there were so few opportunities available to second-generation Chinese Americans. Wong had graduated from Mills College, but she noticed that none of the other Chinese Americans from her high school had gone to college. "On account of economic pressures," explained a Chinese American woman in 1941, "the majority of second generation Chinese are forced to give up their studies after they finish high school. Most of their fathers are either restaurant keepers or laundry-men whose income is too small for sending children to colleges and universities."

The second-generation Chinese did not want to fol-low their parents to a lifetime of work in "chop-suey houses and laundries." They hated working in Chinatown and being limited to the traditional Chinese trades. They wanted to break away from the immigrant status of their parents and hoped that education and better jobs would advance them toward equality in American society. Some second-generation Chinese managed to pursue their educations, but progress toward equality remained slow. Even with college degrees, they could not find work in the higher-paying jobs and fields of their choices. Seeking to be judged on the basis of merit, they found that employers judged them on the basis of race.

"Even if you had an education, there was no other work than in a laundry or restaurant," explained the owner of a laundry in New York. When a student at Stanford Univer-sity applied for a job as a chauffeur for a retired banker and his wife, he was asked, "You Chinee boy or Jap boy?" Amazed, he replied, "Chinese, of course, but born in this country." The banker's wife then told him, "Me no likee, me no wantee

Chinee boy." Seized with a "huge desire to laugh" at her effort to speak to him in pidgin English, he burst out, "Mrs. Bitterns, I understand perfectly."

Two Chinese engineers wrote to 50 engineering companies applying for positions. They received only rejections. A young man who graduated from the University of Southern California with a degree in electrical engineering in 1923 told a researcher in 1925, "I have tried to get into the engineering field but thus far have not been able to do so." After failing to find a job as an engineer, a Chinese graduate of the Massachusetts Institute of Technology (MIT) became a waiter in a Chinese restaurant. In a prize-winning essay called "Does My Future Lie in China or America," a Harvard University student wrote in 1936 that his brother, a graduate of MIT, did not get a single job offer, although he wrote many letters of application.

The Great Depression of the 1930s made matters worse for the second-generation Chinese because so many whites were looking for jobs at the same time. A young Chinese American asked, "With thousands of fair-minded, blue-eyed collegians at his elbows, looking for a job, with thousands of similar tinted fellows working for a raise, ready to take his place the moment he slips, is there a chance for a person with a yellow skin?"

Prospects for Chinese Americans were generally discouraging. In 1927, the executive secretary of the YWCA in San Francisco told a Stanford University researcher, "The employment situation is very difficult for the Chinese, particularly for the American born Chinese, trained in the schools here. There are so few openings for the Chinese in the line of work he or she may have trained. If there is an opening,

preference is, of course, given to the white applicant regardless of ability."

The registrar of San Francisco State College told a student that she could enroll in a course. "But after the course," the registrar candidly added, "don't expect to be placed [in a job], because you are Chinese." Sometimes Chinese graduates did get jobs, but they were paid less than whites. A Stanford graduate was considered for a job by an American company: "The manager was willing to pay him $5,000 a year but one of his business associates said, '$4,000 is good enough. After all, he is a Chinese.'"

The second generation of Chinese Americans wondered whether they could make a life outside Chinatown.

Chinese American volunteers served in the U.S. Army in World War I (1914–18).

93

Most young Chinese workers were trapped in an ethnic and low-skilled labor market. Chinese girls could get jobs in stores as stock handlers, working in storerooms behind the scenes, but not as salespeople dealing with the public. Chinese women could get jobs as cigarette girls if they wore Chinese dresses; they were sometimes hired to add "atmosphere" in theater lobbies when a Charlie Chan movie was showing. In 1938, the Oriental Division of the United States Employment Service in San Francisco reported that 90% of the jobs it found for Chinese workers were in services, chiefly as cooks or waiters. The report added that most firms discriminated against the Chinese, even well-educated Chinese who were U.S. citizens.

Young Chinese in San Francisco seemed to have "no future worthy of their education." They were destined instead to "washing dishes, carrying trays, ironing shirts, cutting meat, drying fish, and selling herbs." They encountered racial prejudice from interviewers, employers, and co-workers, who told

The Great Depression of the 1930s brought hardship to Americans of all ethnic backgrounds. Unemployed Chinese workers joined a 1933 hunger march in Sacramento, California, asking the state legislature for unemployment benefits.

them, "Go back to Chinatown where you belong." American-born Chinese women were discriminated against for two reasons: because they were women, and because they were Chinese. With help from her Catholic church, a Chinese woman got a job as a file clerk in a San Francisco insurance company in the 1920s. "You have no right here," some whites told her. "By rights you should be in Chinatown, doing laundry."

Seeing how they were discriminated against in the job market, some second-generation Chinese wondered whether they could have a future in the United States. A Chinese newspaper in San Francisco felt that they could not. It advised them to go to China: "In the fields of agriculture and aviation, China is much lacking in Western knowledge. Unlimited opportunities are ahead. . . . Indeed, your future lies with China, not with America."

In China, they would not have to worry about being rejected for a job because they were Chinese. A University of Washington student complained that the better jobs and career advancement were not available to him in "this fair land." He thought about going "across the Pacific and to China." A Chinese woman at Stanford University said in 1924, "The Chinese who are trained in the schools here do not expect to remain in the United States, but they are looking toward China for the future." Some Chinese Americans actually did "return" to China.

"We *were* all immigrants in those days, no matter where we were born," recalled a Chinese American man bitterly. "Between the Chinese and the English education, we had no idea where we belonged. Even to this day, if I wanted to say, 'I'm going to China,' I would never say it that way; I would say '*go back* to China.' Because I was taught from the time I was born that this was not my country, that I would have to go to China to make my living as an adult."

The second-generation Chinese plainly saw their problem: They "looked Chinese." Yet America was their country. Citizens by birth, they had attended American schools, and many had even graduated from college. As citizens, they expected to have greater opportunities available to them. But as they saw the racial barriers erected against them, they woke up from this "illusion." Many were disappointed, depressed, and angry. Some found satisfaction in turning to their ethnic roots, insisting they were "very proud to belong to the Chinese race." Some decided to struggle for their rights as citizens, while others gave up their hopes of becoming full and equal citizens. But whatever their response to racial rejection, all of them felt they were strangers in America.

Chinese people in America had known for a long time that the way they were treated in the United States was tied to political developments in China. The weakness of the Chinese government in the late 19th and early 20th centuries made it easier for the U.S. government to impose its anti-immigration laws. If the government of China had been stronger in world politics, the United States would have been less willing to offend it by refusing entry to Chinese immigrants.

For this reason, the Chinese population in America took a keen interest in affairs back in China. Chinese Americans supported China's struggle for independence from foreign powers. They hoped that a strong and independent China would mean greater protection and more rights for them in the United States. But they watched in grief and dismay as

their homeland was victimized by other nations, including
Japan. In a war between the two nations in 1894–95, China
was humiliated by Japan. Ten years later, Japan defeated
Russia in a war in Siberia; this strengthened Japanese influence
in China. Then, during the 1930s, Chinese people in the
United States watched Japan reveal its plan for control of
China. On September 18, 1931, the Japanese army attacked
northern China. Five months later, Japan violently seized the
Chinese port city of Shanghai.

As they witnessed the terrible acts of Japanese aggres-
sion, the second-generation Chinese felt a surge of national-
ism, a deep concern for the homeland of their parents. In
Chinese school they listened to the principal give speeches
about how Chinese leaders should do more to fight the
Japanese. Each event in the Japanese takeover of China became
another humiliation for Chinese Americans. "If you were
Chinese American, you certainly felt the fate of China was
important," recalled one man. "I remember the teachers would
always complain, 'China is weak, and look at the treatment
we get here.'"

But international developments were exploding that
would influence the future of the Chinese in American society.
When Jade Snow Wong graduated from Mills College, she
worried about her career plans. She had assumed she would
enter graduate studies for a master's degree in social work.
"But Pearl Harbor had been bombed," she wrote in her
autobiography, "and the students, like everyone else, were
caught in the war fever."

Just as the San Francisco earthquake had changed the
course of history for the first generation of Chinese Americans, World War II changed history for a later generation.

*In 1938, 15,000 Chinese
residents of New York
marched to protest Japan's
invasion of China and to
show support for the battle for
freedom in their homeland.*

After Japan bombed Pearl Harbor in Hawaii in December 1941, the United States entered the war. China and the United States were allies against Japan. Suddenly, Chinese people in America found themselves viewed as friends, while Japanese Americans were seen as enemies. Remembering how they had often been called "Japs," Chinese people took pains not to be mistaken for Japanese. Signs went up in store windows: "This is a Chinese shop." People wore buttons that said, "I am Chinese."

Chinese Americans made important contributions to the war effort. They joined the armed forces, worked in aircraft and weapons plants, and bought war bonds. Thousands of laundrymen, waiters, and garment workers finally had a chance to break out of the ethnic economy of Chinatown; as the war continued and the defense industries grew desperate for workers, they got jobs in shipyards and factories. Jade Snow Wong, who could not find a job after leaving school, got her secretarial post in a navy shipyard at this time.

Sharing the war effort, young Chinese Americans felt a new closeness to the United States. A young man from San Francisco's Chinatown said, "World War II was the most important historical event of our times. For the first time we felt we could make it in American society." A resident of New York's Chinatown explained, "In the 1940s for the first time Chinese were accepted by Americans as being friends because at that time, Chinese and Americans were fighting against the Japanese and the Germans and the Nazis. Therefore, all of a sudden, we became part of an American dream."

The improved status of the Chinese was finally recognized in law. Under pressure from its allies in China and from Chinese Americans at home, the U.S. Congress ended the long ban on immigration from China in 1943. In fact, the change in the law allowed only a tiny trickle of immigration from China: no more than 105 Chinese could enter each year. The law also opened the way to citizenship. Chinese immigrants living in the United States could now apply to become naturalized U.S. citizens—if they could prove that they had entered the country legally; they also had to pass tests in their ability to use the English language and their knowledge of American history and the U.S. Constitution.

One of the 1,428 Chinese immigrants who won their citizenship between 1944 and 1952 was Jade Snow Wong's father. "At the age of seventy plus, after years of attending night classes in citizenship, he became naturalized," his daughter joyfully reported. "He embraced this status wholeheartedly. One day when we were discussing plans for his birthday celebration, which was usually observed on the tenth day of the fifth lunar month by the Chinese calendar, he announced, 'Now that I have become a United States citizen,

Chinese American women—like many other women in the United States—found new roles during World War II. They went to work in factories, doing jobs that had formerly been done by the men who had been called to the front.

I am going to change my birthday. Henceforth, it will be on the Fourth of July.'"

Good relations between the United States and China did not last long after the war ended in 1945. China was plunged into civil war between communist and noncommunist forces, and in 1949, the communists under the leadership of Mao Zedong won control of the country and established a communist state called the People's Republic of China, while the former rulers of China fled to the island of Taiwan. The United States refused to recognize the People's Republic of China, and contact broke off between the two nations.

These developments in China splintered Chinese communities in America. Chinese American intellectuals who were sympathetic to communism, as well as workers' associations, cheered Mao's triumph. Other groups, such as the Chinese Six Companies, supported the campaign to overthrow communist rule in mainland China.

In 1950, the People's Republic of China became involved in the Korean War. This set off hysterical anti-

Chinese reactions in the United States. Many white Americans, fearful of the spread of Asian communism, imagined a new peril in their own communities. A Chinese American woman recalled those days: "The Korean War affected us at the beginning in that we were taken for Communists. People would look at you in the street and think, 'Well, you're one of the enemy.'"

"The whole atmosphere here then was fear," a Chinese American man explained. "If you weren't careful, you could be thrown into a concentration camp." In late 1950, Congress passed the McCarran Internal Security Act, which said that communists could be rounded up and sent to camps during a national emergency. This law was an ominous and menacing reminder to the Chinese in America. During World War II, Japanese Americans on the West Coast had been sent to concentration camps. Now, in the Cold War between the communists and their enemies, the same thing could happen to Chinese Americans. They were forced to prove their loyalty to the United States.

To show that not all Chinese were communists, the Chinese Six Companies of San Francisco and the Chinese Benevolent Association of New York led anticommunist campaigns in Chinatowns across the country. In 1951, the newly formed Anti-Communist Committee for Free China declared its full loyalty to the United States and said that communism was un-Chinese. In 1954, the All-American Overseas Chinese Anti-Communist League was established in New York to reassure white America that the Chinese in America were not communists.

Fear of communism soon threatened to get out of control. In 1955, after an American official in Hong Kong warned that spies from the People's Republic of China could use false citizenship papers to get American passports and enter the United States, U.S. authorities began investigating thousands of Chinese Americans, charging that their passports were based on false birth certificates. As the government prosecuted and deported the Chinese residents who were found guilty of fraud, waves of alarm and fear swept through Chinese communities. The "paper sons," those who had entered the United States with false papers to bypass the ban on Chinese immigration, were especially frightened.

To help in its investigations, the government created the Confession Program. Chinese residents who had entered the United States illegally were encouraged to come forward and confess their guilt to the Immigration and Naturalization Service (INS). They were then required to give details about the status of all their relatives and friends, which meant that a single confession could involve dozens of people. In return for the confessions, the government allowed those who confessed to remain in the country as long as they were not involved in spying or other disloyal activities. Thousands of people participated in the program. In San Francisco alone, 10,000 Chinese confessed. Ninety-nine percent of all confessors were allowed to stay in the United States.

The Confession Program gave the government a weapon to use against Chinese residents who were thought to be undesirable. The INS and the Federal Bureau of Investigation (FBI) used information from the confessions to identify people who supported the communist government in China or who belonged to groups that were considered un-American. These unlucky individuals were sent out of the country. The program spread poisonous divisions and distrust within the

Chinese community. "We knew the FBI was keeping a close eye on us, and we even suspected there was an informer among us," said a man who belonged to the Min Ching, an organization that supported Chinese communism. "I guess that's one thing all of us feel bad about now, that we had to be suspicious of each other." He explained that entire families had to be fearful: "Say, if a Min Ching member is discovered to have false papers, his whole family will be affected because probably they didn't have the proper papers either. So they'll go from you, to the uncle who brought you in, his wife, and it goes on and on."

Gradually, as the anticommunist hysteria died down during the 1960s, pressure on the Chinese residents of the United States was eased. In the mid-1960s, the history of Chinese America entered a new phase. The civil rights movement was gaining strength in the United States, and racism was under attack. Seeking to end racism in the immigration laws, Congress passed a new federal Immigration Act in 1965. Under the new law, 20,000 Chinese immigrants could enter the United States each year. In addition, family members of Chinese people already living in the United States were also free to enter. The result was a massive second wave of Asian immigration.

In the two decades from 1965 to 1985, four times as many Asian immigrants came to America as during the whole previous century. More than one-quarter of those newcomers were Chinese, and many of them flocked to the Chinatowns of American cities.

Young women from Hong Kong, students at California's Mills College, are San Yi Man, "second wave immigrants,"—part of the flood of newcomers that have made the Chinese the third largest group of immigrants in the United States.

THE CHINESE WHO CAME TO AMERICA IN THE SECOND
wave are called the *San Yi Man* ("new immigrants"). They are
the third largest group of immigrants, after Mexicans
and Filipinos. Between 1965 and 1984, they numbered
419,000—almost as many as the 426,000 Chinese who came
to the United States between 1849 and 1930. Their arrival
helped change the ethnic shape of American society. In 1960,
before the second wave of immigration began, the Chinese
population in the United States numbered only 237,000, half
the size of the Japanese population. Twenty years later, the
Chinese population had jumped to 812,200, and there were
more Chinese than Japanese people in the country.

The Chinese community itself had changed. The
flood of newcomers meant that by 1980, nearly two-thirds of
all Chinese people in America had been born in Asia. Once
again, Chinese America was mainly an immigrant community.

More than half of the second-wave Chinese settled
in two states, California and New York. Their presence has
been revitalizing Chinatowns there. New York City, the first
choice of many new Chinese immigrants, has seen a population explosion in its Chinatown. Before the 1965 Immigration
Act, New York's Chinatown never had more than 15,000
people; by 1985, it was home to 100,000.

This tide of new immigrants from China was not
expected at all when Congress passed the 1965 Immigration
Act. The supporters of the law, hoping to promote immigration by white Europeans, had included a provision that gave
preference in the immigration quotas to adult relatives of
people already living in the United States. The idea was that
this provision would encourage the brothers, sisters, and
cousins of immigrants from Europe to come to the United

States. But it also reopened the way for immigrants from China. Explained one of the *San Yi Man:* "My brother-in-law left his wife in Taiwan and came here as a student to get a Ph.D. in engineering. After he received his degree, he got a job in San Jose. Then he brought in a sister and his wife, who brought over one of her brothers and me. And my brother's wife then came."

This family history is typical. During the 1960s, Chinese students began flocking to U.S. colleges and universities. By 1980, half of the 300,000 foreign students in America were from China and other Asian countries. Thousands of Chinese students were able to find jobs, which meant that the Labor Department would consider them immigrants in the category of skilled workers. In this way, large numbers of Chinese were able to change their status from foreign students to immigrants.

Once they had become immigrants, they could expand the network of relatives under the 1965 immigration law. They could bring their wives and children to America. Then, a few years later, once they had become U.S. citizens, both husband and wife could bring their parents. They could then sponsor their brothers and sisters, who, in turn, could arrange for the entry of their own spouses, children, in-laws, and so on. One immigrant, originally coming to the United States as a foreign student, could thus begin a long chain of migrations.

Unlike the first immigrants, who were mostly peasants from the Chinese countryside, the second-wave immigrants came mainly from the cities. They represented not only the working class but also the professional class. Between 1966 and 1975, nearly half of all Chinese immigrants were managers, professionals (including scientists, doctors, and

engineers), and technical workers. Unlike the Gold Mountain Men, they did not come to America planning to work for a few years and then return to the homeland. They were eager to become American citizens. Three-fourths of the Chinese people who entered the United States between 1969 and 1978 became naturalized citizens within eight years.

Gender is an important difference between the first and second waves of Chinese immigration. Most of the first immigrants were men, but the second wave has included more

In an effort to help new arrivals overcome the language barrier, community groups such as the Los Angeles Chinese American Citizens Alliance offer classes in English for adults.

women than men. Fifty-two percent of the Chinese who entered the United States between 1966 and 1975 were female.

Most of the second-wave immigrants fled at first from the People's Republic of China, the communist country on the Chinese mainland. They usually entered the United States from a second point of departure such as the British colony of Hong Kong or the island nation of Taiwan rather than directly from mainland China, although after the United States opened trade with the People's Republic in 1979, the communist state was allowed to have its own immigration quota.

The second-wave immigrants came to America for a variety of reasons. Like many of the first-wave immigrants who fled from the turmoil of civil war in 19th-century China, some of the recent immigrants also sought refuge from political conflict and instability in China. Betty Chu is one of these. After the communists came to power in China in 1949, she accepted the idea of communism and became a high-school teacher. But during the 1960s, she saw that people were beginning to live in fear. People suspected of having anticommunist thoughts were harassed by young communists and sent to remote provinces. Worried about this rising political repression, Chu and her husband made a secret decision to leave China. Her husband got permission to visit his brother in Hong Kong and then stayed there; Chu followed with her son. Her husband's brother had gone to the United States as a student years earlier and had become an American citizen. He sponsored the Chu family as immigrants in 1969.

Another second-wave immigrant, Xiu Zhen, was less fortunate. She was also a high-school teacher in China, and she was accused of being a spy. "Maybe I wrote some letters and mentioned something political," she explained later, "but I was not political at all." Her hair was cut off and she was put in jail. "Everybody was placed in this one room," she said. "I was there about one year and two months with fourteen other people. We didn't sleep there. We went home at night, but they made us work very hard. . . . Sometimes the Red Guards burned me with cigarettes. They kept saying, 'We have to wash your brains.'" In 1974, Xiu was allowed to visit her mother in Hong Kong. "I said I had to go to her because she was sick. Of course that was not the real reason." From Hong Kong, she came to the United States.

Like the 19th-century pioneers who sought Gold Mountain, some second-wave Chinese immigrants were pulled to America by the hope of a brigher, more prosperous future. "The people told me that coming to America will be just great," said an immigrant who arrived in 1968. "There was hot running water, cold water and even warm air [heating]. The water in the village countryside was filthy and very unsanitary, filled with pigs' and other animals' waste. Any place with 'clean water' must be like 'the sky above the sky.' America is 'Heaven.'"

The immigrants of the second wave saw America as a place of possibilities. Wing Ng came to the United States in 1975 at the age of 23. "The reason why I wanted to come to the United States is that I heard it is really freedom," she said. "That's the first thing. And the second was education." Wing joined her father in Hong Kong, but she found that her opportunities for work and education there were extremely limited: "In Hong Kong it is difficult to go to college, too. Only two universities. Too many people. Too much competition for jobs. The people in Hong Kong don't like the others coming in and taking the jobs. So the only jobs you can get are in the factories."

America would be a land of greater opportunity, the *San Yi Man* believed. But when they arrived, they found impoverished Chinatowns in cities like San Francisco and New York. Shrouded behind the tourist image of Chinatown as a charming and colorful community was the reality of the ghetto: poverty, unemployment, and crowded housing. The immigrants also faced economic discrimination. In 1960,

Many new immigrants, especially those who do not yet speak English, work in low-paying jobs without benefits or job security.

Chinese male workers in New York City and San Francisco earned only about 56 to 68 cents for every dollar earned by white male workers. Chinese women fared even worse, earning less than half as much as white women.

The unemployment rate for men in San Francisco's Chinatown was almost 13%, nearly double the 7% rate for the city as a whole. Chinatown was also crowded, with 885 people per residential acre, compared with only 82 people per acre in the other sections of the city. In New York's Chinatown, more than a third of all families lived below the official poverty level. More than half of the housing units in both Chinatowns were old and run-down. Both communities had extremely high rates of suicide and tuberculosis. Many inhabitants were elderly men, "bachelors" from the first wave of immigration, living out the remainder of their lives in tiny rooms in shabby hotels.

The different class backgrounds of the old and new immigrants has led to a division within the Chinese-American community, between working-class menial laborers and educated, middle-class professionals. New York City has the "Downtown Chinese," who are mostly waiters and seamstresses, and also the wealthier "Uptown Chinese." In southern California, there are Chinatowns in central Los Angeles and also in more prosperous suburbs like Monterey Park.

Monterey Park has been called "America's first suburban Chinatown." It is a striking contrast to the old urban Chinatowns. The Chinese have become the largest ethnic group in Monterey Park, totaling more than half of the 61,000 residents in 1988. During the early 1980s, the city elected its first Chinese mayor, Lilly Chen. But not everyone welcomed the new Chinese presence. In 1986, for example, a sign at a gas station near the city limits showed two slanted eyes and the words: "Will the last American to leave Monterey Park please bring the flag."

The Chinese residents of Monterey Park are not allowing such bigotry to discourage them. They are building an American city in their image, and they can afford to do so. Many of the city's Chinese residents are wealthy; Chinese real estate agents call Monterey Park a "Chinese Beverly Hills," and BMWs and other expensive cars are parked on the streets. The Chinese own two-thirds of the property and businesses in the city. Monterey Park has Chinese markets, restaurants, and retail stores as well as Chinese theaters, churches, doctors, and lawyers. It is a complete Chinese community.

But most of the second-wave immigrants have gathered in the old urban Chinatowns. More than three-fourths of the people in New York, San Francisco, and Los Angeles Chinatowns are foreign-born. Unlike the suburban Chinese professionals, they are mostly low-wage laborers. Most of them do not have even a high-school degree. They also lack English language skills; more than half of the Chinese residents of New York's Chinatown speak English poorly or not at all. "This does not mean that they are not trying to learn," explains a community organizer. "In fact, there are at least two dozen English-language schools in the community. . . . Thousands of working people squeeze time out from their busy schedules to attend classes. However, the real problem is that they do not have the opportunity to use English on the job or with other Chinese immigrants. They soon forget the scant English they have learned."

Poor English skills and limited job opportunities make for a vicious cycle. "Chinese people have lower incomes

because first, the language problem," says a second-wave immigrant. "If you know just a little English, you can go to an office and get a job cleaning up. It has more security, more benefits. But how are you going to get a job like that if you don't know a little English? And how are you going to learn English if you have to work twelve hours a day, six days a week and then come home and take care of your family?"

Unable to speak English, many Chinese immigrant women have no choice but to work as seamstresses. A study of garment workers in San Francisco Chinatown found that nearly three-quarters of them are secondary wage earners. They have husbands who work—but they have to work too, to help the family barely get by. Yet most of these women are still solely responsible for all household chores. With this double burden, they must look for jobs in the garment indus-

The tide of new immigrants has caused a population boom in New York City's crowded Chinatown.

113

try, where they can have flexible work hours and can bring their babies to sleep near them in the factory.

While women are located largely in the garment industry, men are employed mainly in the restaurants. The director of an English-language school in San Francisco Chinatown explains how recent immigrants are locked into low-paying restaurant jobs: "Most immigrants coming into Chinatown with a language barrier cannot go outside this

In Chinatown's hotels and apartment buildings, elderly men from the first wave of immigration live out their lives. Meanwhile, the immigrants of the second wave are bringing new vitality to urban Chinese America.

confined area into the mainstream of American industry." One man who had recently arrived in the United States said, "Before I was a painter in Hong Kong, but I can't do it here. I got no license, no education. . . . I want a living, so it's dishwasher, janitor or cook."

Many of the recent immigrants who were professionals in their home countries have had to take menial jobs in America. "There are innumerable instances of former doctors, teachers, accountants, and engineers who took jobs as janitors and waiters when they first arrived," said one woman. "Some stay in the rut because of language problems or because they are afraid to venture out and compete vigorously in the job market." One couple held teaching jobs in China: the wife was a mathematics teacher and the husband was a professor of Chinese at a university. In San Francisco, however, she works as an office clerk and he as a janitor in a hotel. Both of them want to get ahead. Each night they study English until two in the morning.

Wei-Chi Poon and her husband, Boon Pui Poon, also experienced the problem of underemployment. Before they came to America in 1968, she was a biology professor and he was an architect in the People's Republic of China. "We had a really hard time right after we got here," she reported. "My husband was a very good architect, but because he couldn't speak English he could work only as a draftsman. His pay was so low that he had to work at two jobs, from eight in the morning till eleven o'clock at night." She worked in a laundry factory, packing uniforms into bags to be sent to Vietnam and earning only the minimum wage of $1.85 an hour. "The bags were at least 100 pounds each. At the time, I was one of the younger workers, so I had more strength than some of the

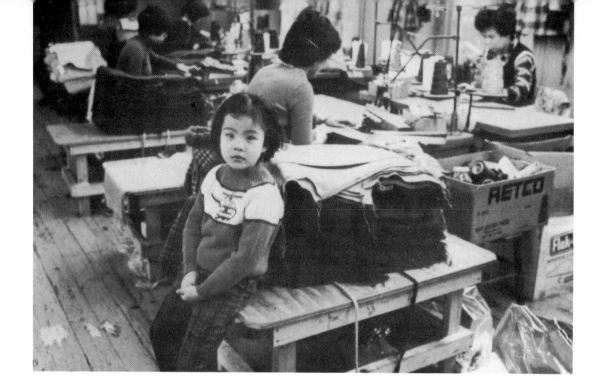

others. I got scared, wondering, 'Will I be doing this for the rest of my life?'"

She knew she would be trapped unless she learned English—but, as she said, "We were so busy working and so tired we had no time and energy to study English." A program funded by the Comprehensive Employment Training Act let her take English classes while working as a library assistant in the Chinatown branch of the San Francisco Library. She enrolled in the city's junior college and went on to do graduate study in library science. Now Wei-Chi Poon is head of the Asian American Studies Library of the University of California.

The children of the second-wave Chinese face special difficulties and challenges. They feel confined in Chinatown, aware of the boundaries that limit their lives and their parents' lives. English is their second language, spoken outside the home. They also feel a strong obligation to do well in school, particularly to please their parents. They are often reminded by their parents, especially the college-educated parents who were professionals in China and Taiwan, that education is the key to advancement in America. "Yes, with a good education, my children can find a better job," explained a Chinese mother, who had a college degree from a university in China and worked in a factory in the United States. "I don't want them to be like the first generation of Chinese immigrants here. They have to work so hard in those slave labor jobs."

The second-wave Chinese immigrants differ from earlier immigrants in many ways, but they often encounter the same prejudice and rejection that made the first immigrants feel that they were "eating bitterness." One immigrant student in Los Angeles told of insults from her white fellow students: "American students always picked on us, frightened us, made fun of us and laughed at our English. They broke our lockers, threw food on us in the cafeteria, said dirty words to us, pushed us on campus. Many times they shouted at me, 'Get out of here, you chink, go back to your country.'"

Like the Gold Mountain Men who came to California in the 19th century, the new Chinese immigrants have found themselves treated as strangers in America. Yet they continue to cross the sea to America, hoping to fulfill their dreams of work, school, family life, and community. They are keeping the urban Chinatowns alive, creating a Chinese American presence in the suburbs and universities, and helping to shape multicultural America.

Chronology

1790	A federal law says that only "white" immigrants may become naturalized citizens of the United States.
1849	The California Gold Rush begins with the arrival of prospectors called "Forty-Niners," including 325 Chinese.
1865–69	Chinese laborers build the transcontinental railroad.
1868	The Burlingame Treaty between the United States and China guarantees protection for the civil rights of Chinese people in America.
1870	The federal Civil Rights Act improves the legal status of the Chinese in America.
1882	The U.S. Congress passes the Chinese Exclusion Act, which prevents Chinese laborers from entering the United States.
1884	A U.S. court bans the immigration of Chinese women in the *Ah Moy* case.
1906	The San Francisco earthquake destroys immigration records, making it possible for more Chinese immigrants to enter the country.

1910	An immigration station is established at Angel Island, California.
1924	The federal Immigration Act cuts off immigration from Asian countries.
1933	The Chinese Hand Laundry Alliance (CHLA) is formed in New York to combat discrimination against Chinese laundry operators.
1941	The United States enters World War II.
1943	The U.S. Congress ends the ban on immigration from China and allows the Chinese to become naturalized citizens.
1945	World War II ends.
1949	The People's Republic of China is established by Chinese communists.
1950	The People's Republic of China enters the Korean War, causing a surge of anticommunist and anti-Chinese feeling in the United States; Congress passes the McCarran Internal Security Act, which would allow communists to be placed in concentration camps.
1965	The Immigration Act of 1965 opens the door for a second great wave of Asian immigration.

Further Reading

Chan, Sucheng. *Asian Americans: An Interpretive History.* Boston: Twayne, 1991.

Chen, Jack. *The Chinese of America: From the Beginnings to the Present.* New York: Harper & Row, 1981.

Chinn, Thomas, H. M. Lai, and Philip Choy. *A History of the Chinese in California.* New York: Chinese Historical Society, 1981.

Chu, Louis. *Eat a Bowl of Tea.* Secaucus, NJ: Lyle Stuart, 1974.

Daley, William. *The Chinese Americans.* New York: Chelsea House, 1987.

Gee, Emma, ed. *Asian Women.* Berkeley: Asian American Studies Center, University of California, 1971.

Gillenkirk, Jeff, and James Motlow. *Bitter Melon: Stories from the Last Rural Chinese Town in America.* Seattle: University of Washington Press, 1987.

Hoexter, Corinne K. *From Canton to California: The Epic of Chinese Immigration.* New York: Four Winds, 1976.

Hom, Marlon K., ed. and trans. *Songs of Gold Mountain: Cantonese Rhymes from San Francisco Chinatown.* Berkeley: University of California Press, 1987.

Jones, Claire. *The Chinese in America.* Minneapolis: Lerner Publications, 1972.

Kingston, Maxine Hong. *The Woman Warrior*. New York: Vintage, 1977.

Lai, Him Mark, Joe Huang, and Don Wong. *The Chinese of America, 1795–1980*. San Francisco: Chinese Culture Foundation, 1980.

Lai, Him Mark, Genny Lim, and Judy Yung, eds. *Island: Poetry and History of Chinese Immigrants on Angel Island*. San Francisco: Chinese Culture Foundation, 1980.

Lee, Gus. *China Boy*. New York: Dutton, 1991.

McCunn, Ruthanne Lum. *Chinese American Portraits: Personal Histories, 1828–1988*. San Francisco: Chronicle Books, 1988.

Mark, Diane Mei Lin, and Ginger Chih. *A Place Called Chinese America*. Dubuque, IA: Kendall/Hunt, 1982.

———. *Thousand Pieces of Gold*. San Francisco: Design Enterprises, 1981.

Nee, Victor, and Brett de Barry Nee. *Longtime Californ': A Documentary Study of an American Chinatown*. Boston: Houghton Mifflin, 1974.

Ng, Fay. *Bone*. New York: Hyperion Press, 1993.

Perrin, Linda. *Coming to America: Immigrants from the Far East*. New York: Delacorte Press, 1980.

Reimers, David M. *The Immigrant Experience*. New York: Chelsea House, 1989.

Takaki, Ronald. *A Different Mirror: A History of Multicultural America*. Boston: Little, Brown, 1993.

————. *From Different Shores: Perspectives on Race and Ethnicity in America.* New York: Oxford University Press, 1987.

Tan, Amy. *The Joy Luck Club.* New York: Putnam, 1989.

Telemaque, Eleanore Wong. *It's Crazy To Stay Chinese in Minnesota.* Nashville: Thomas Nelson, 1978.

Tsai, Shih-Shan Henry. *The Chinese Experience in America.* Bloomington: Indiana University Press, 1986.

Yung, Judy. *Chinese Women of America: A Pictorial History.* Seattle: University of Washington Press, 1986.

Wong, Jade Snow. *Fifth Chinese Daughter.* New York: Harper & Row, 1945.

Index

PICTURE CREDITS

RONALD TAKAKI, the son of immigrant plantation laborers from Japan, graduated from the College of Wooster, Ohio, and earned his Ph.D. in history from the University of California at Berkeley, where he has served both as the chairperson and the graduate advisor of the Ethnic Studies program. Professor Takaki has lectured widely on issues relating to ethnic studies and multiculturalism in the United States, Japan, and the former Soviet Union and has won several important awards for his teaching efforts. He is the author of six books, including the highly acclaimed *Strangers from a Different Shore: A History of Asian Americans,* and the recently published *A Different Mirror: A History of Multicultural America.*

REBECCA STEFOFF is a writer and editor who has published more than 50 nonfiction books for young adults. Many of her books deal with geography and exploration, including the three-volume set *Extraordinary Explorers,* recently published by Oxford University Press. Stefoff also takes an active interest in environmental issues. She served as editorial director for two Chelsea House series—*Peoples and Places of the World* and *Let's Discover Canada.* Stefoff studied English at the University of Pennsylvania, where she taught for three years. She lives in Portland, Oregon.